REBOUND

REBOUND

*A Proven Plan for Starting Over
After Job Loss*

Martha I. Finney

Vice President, Publisher: Tim Moore
Associate Publisher and Director of Marketing: Amy Neidlinger
Acquisitions Editor: Jennifer Simon
Editorial Assistant: Pamela Boland
Operations Manager: Gina Kanouse
Digital Marketing Manager: Julie Phifer
Publicity Manager: Laura Czaja
Assistant Marketing Manager: Megan Colvin
Cover Designer: Chuti Prasertsith
Managing Editor: Kristy Hart
Project Editor: Anne Goebel
Copy Editor: Keith Cline
Proofreader: San Dee Phillips
Indexer: Erika Millen
Interior Designer: Bumpy Design
Compositor: Nonie Ratcliff
Manufacturing Buyer: Dan Uhrig

© 2009 by Pearson Education, Inc.
Publishing as FT Press
Upper Saddle River, New Jersey 07458

FT Press offers excellent discounts on this book when ordered in quantity for bulk purchases or special sales. For more information, please contact U.S. Corporate and Government Sales, 1-800-382-3419, corpsales@pearsontechgroup.com. For sales outside the U.S., please contact International Sales at international@pearson.com.

Company and product names mentioned herein are the trademarks or registered trademarks of their respective owners.

Printed in the United States of America

First Printing January 2009

ISBN-10: 0-13-702114-3
ISBN-13: 978-0-13-702114-7

Pearson Education LTD
Pearson Education Australia PTY, Limited.
Pearson Education Singapore, Pte. Ltd.
Pearson Education North Asia, Ltd.
Pearson Education Canada, Ltd.
Pearson Educación de Mexico, S.A. de C.V.
Pearson Education—Japan
Pearson Education Malaysia, Pte. Ltd.

Library of Congress Cataloging-in-Publication Data is available upon request.

To the memory of my father, Richard Anson Finney, and his passionate devotion to his work.

"It's the detours that help us remember who we are."
—Sheryl Crow

Contents

Acknowledgments

Now I know the meaning of the expression *last but not least*. I wish this were a magic page that would discern who is holding this book, and then reshuffle the names so that person's name is listed first. Everyone mentioned here played a crucial part in the creation of this book and the process of putting it in your hands. I barely know how to begin. But I'll give it a shot.

Thanks to Colleen Cayes, as usual and always, for keeping me confident and sane as I plowed ahead under a tight deadline. And, to the newest New Mexican, Katie Wacek, thank you for being here, sharing your stories, perspectives, and insights. I'm so glad that you and Scott moved to Albuquerque! Whatever the circumstances that brought you here, you're here!

And thanks to Lillian Maland, my oldest friend, for our early-morning email routine. I cherish our e-chats.

Thanks to Libby Gill (my new traveling companion, especially in the Robert Louis Stevenson sense), Deborah "Sports Diva" Sullivan, and Jeffrey Saltzman for opening up your stupendous networks to me.

Merry and Derra! To the Hearts! My favorite biweekly date. I just love you two!

Thanks to all the experts who so generously shared their knowledge and insights with me! And my deep appreciation goes to all those who opened their hearts and trusted me with the stories of one of the hardest times of their lives. I'd name you one by one, but I promised you that I wouldn't. But you know who you are. I'm holding your names in my head and heart as I write this.

Thanks to the ab-fab Pearson team, starting with Jennifer Simon, who gave me the challenge assignment of my life. Wow! What a ride you put me on when you called me in Santa Barbara last year! My friends think I was nuts to do it, but I'm so glad I said yes! To Laura Czaja, Megan Colvin, Anne Goebel, and the entire team who started getting the buzz out before I barely had time to turn on the computer.

And, so, last but not least, to Keith Cline, my new friend from the Snowy Mountains. You may have left the judiciary, but I'm so grateful for your judicious hand and sensitive ear. You got it. So I got to keep it. So I get to say thanks!

About the Author

Martha Finney, President and CEO of Engagement Journeys, LLC, is an expert in employee engagement and leadership communications. A business journalist for 20 years before becoming a full-time consultant, she specializes in helping organizations achieve greater employee engagement, loyalty, retention, and passion. Finney is author or coauthor of more than 13 books, including *The Truth About Getting the Best from People* (FT Press), and *HR from the Heart*, with Yahoo's Chief People Officer, Libby Sartain. Her original research on the American workplace has been featured on CNN, NPR's Morning Edition, and in major newspapers nationwide.

Contact her at martha@reboundyourcareer.com

For more information, visit www.reboundyourcareer.com

Preface

We're all human. And because we're all human, we share the habit of marking the moments that change our lives forever. The majority of those moments are cause for celebration (or at least track predictably along what we consider to be nature's plan): births, birthdays, graduations, weddings, babies, grandbabies, even the gentle, timely passing of dearly loved ones, are all cause for noticing and remembering.

But we also mark the times when everything we took for granted goes to chaos and yet another illusion is shattered. Those can be private tragedies or national catastrophes that rock our world and in a twinkling send us hurtling into the next phase of our lives. From the Baby Boom generation and moving forward into the Y generation, we have more in common than we might think we do. And that is this: We're constantly being reminded that nothing is certain. And, come to find out, promises are made to be broken. Huh, what do you know?

The biggest promise that has been repeatedly broken in the past 30 years has been that the "system" (whatever *that* is) is airtight, foolproof, and self-perpetuating. A net of stability we can depend on if we simply walk the straight and narrow. Follow all the rules, make a plan and stick to it, go to college, pour heart and soul into your job, go above and beyond the call to make yourself indispensable, and you'll be fine. That path leads to security. No? Oh. There goes another illusion.

Of course, every generation has had its share of troubles, and we'd be major babies to whine that we've gotten the raw end of the historic deal. I would choose these times over any prior era right this very moment. No question. However, for me, "these times" began in 1977—six months before I was due to graduate from college—when my father came home unexpectedly from an assignment abroad. After more than 25 years with the Central Intelligence Agency as an undercover case officer, he was in the middle of teaching a class in Mexico City when a rap on the glass door delivered a pink slip into his astonished hands. *Adios, muchacho.* Or as his students cooperatively called him, Señor Feingold.

From my perspective—self-absorbed and involved with school-work—he had merely come home ahead of schedule. But he left for work the very next morning, so nothing otherwise was out of ordinary. I would learn later that he had a meeting with an outplacement counselor his first day back. Incredibly, the counselor observed, "You seem angry, Mr. Finney." (As if *that* were going to pry open a "cleansing" outpouring of emotions from a guy who kept secrets for a living.) If my dad were a member of a younger generation, he would have said, "Damn straight, I'm pissed." But instead, he rose to his feet, walked out the door, turning his back on his life's passion, mission, and calling. Why not? His life's passion, mission, and calling had turned its back on him.

That happened right after a period when my father was anxiously and responsibly giving me the advice to choose a "recession-proof" career, and that meant—to his loyal way of thinking—a job with the federal government. But, as I was to read later, he was a member of the first of many waves of federal layoffs, called Reduction in Force. Thousands upon thousands of federal employees were to be tossed out of work during the Carter and Reagan administrations. So much for working for the feds. There goes another promise broken.

He spent the next year or so unsuccessfully trying to land another job. (I mean, how transferrable *are* the skills you learn in more than 25 years as a spy? Especially when you can't actually say what you were doing all those years? Talk about a resumé gap.) After some ridiculous misfires in industrial security, one of which was as a security guard for a movie about New York thugs, which caused him to become an actual victim of a garden-variety mugging on the deserted Coney Island subway platform (there's little more pitiful than an aging ex-spy with broken glasses and a bloodied nose), he eventually settled down to become an international political consultant with his former boss—who had also been shown the door.

But the moment I will always remember is the moment just weeks after my college graduation when he finally admitted to me that he had actually been laid off. Wait a minute! What? I had heard of layoffs before, of course, but they happened to *other people*—especially people who couldn't keep up with the times, who couldn't nimbly retool themselves fast enough to stay ahead of the axe, people who hadn't taken care of themselves by getting a lot of education, making a plan and sticking to it, going above and beyond the call to make themselves indispensable so that they would be fine. Now this was happening to a dedicated, college-educated, multilingual *genius* (he was my father, after all) who over decades had more than demonstrated his immediate value to his company's mission-critical objectives.

Being my father's daughter, I took the news evenly, with no overt reaction of shock, or any sign of the seismic shift that extended from my brain and down through my body and deep into my own future. But that very moment, I came to the instant understanding that no matter who I worked for, I would always and only be working for myself (a conclusion that 20 years later would be echoed in the title of a book by Cliff Hakim, *We Are All Self-Employed*—or as my father's Mexican students might one day be destined to read in their own round of dismissals, *Todos Somos Autoempleados*).

That was the moment that changed my life forever.

I laid myself off right then and there. Oh, I tried off and on throughout the ensuing years to go legit and get and actually keep a full-time job. But I kept returning to a truth that I understood at a most cellular level: The system is whack. Every time I depended on one source for my livelihood, I couldn't shake the feeling that my own personal employment crisis was one decision away.

That was also the moment that handed me my own life's assignment—to write about the world of employment. My father's pain became my calling. I have since spent my career, the past 20 years especially, focusing on how people can marry their talents, passion, and sense of personal mission with truly sensible career management. Which puts me in an exquisitely perfect position to be the one to write this book.

At this point, for most of us, the actual concept of layoffs isn't quite the sucker punch it was to my father's generation. My generation and all of you who are younger have been exposed to layoffs, downsizing, rightsizing, and so on, in some way or another. Either your parents faced it, your friends' parents, or your parents' friends. Or your friends. Or you.

Unless you have been completely in denial, you know that there is no such thing as the job-for-life contract. Hasn't been for decades. We come to this new world with the ironic advantage of knowing full well that the axe could fall, completely out of the blue, for no reason whatsoever.

Still, that doesn't make it any easier when it happens to you or the ones you love, does it?

And this time, the lack of control and chaos seem to have ratcheted up several notches. As I write this Preface, the economy is in freefall, and the headline crawl at the bottom of my TV screen has just announced another loss of 240,000 jobs. Layoffs are everywhere, saturating communities or picking off individual households here and there while skipping over entire blocks.

And it's impossible to track the craziness behind rounds of dismissals. Highly educated, high performers, even high producers are being shown the door. You know who you are. You're the one who is educated; you tooled your skillset according to your passions and according to what all the magazines predicted would be the hot careers of the new century. You've been smart, you've been strategic, in every single step and decision you made in the construction of your career, your profession.

You knew your job, you loved your job. And you did it well. The system wasn't supposed to play out like this, was it? But it did. And now here you are, holding this book in your hands. *This* book! Damn!

So what can you hope to get from these pages? A plan of action and understanding into how to build your entire life from here on out.

Getting laid off is more than just a career crisis. It touches every aspect of your life—your finances, certainly, your health, your emotional health, your relationships, your legal considerations, your future, your identity and self-esteem, even the future of your children and their ability to aspire to a happy life.

No one person can cover all this territory. Fortunately, over the past 20 years or so of writing about this stuff, I've made some very smart friends whose collective wisdom will give you the insights you need to take the next steps wisely. This book represents a gathering of some of the best minds in their respective fields. I have reached out to my network, and all my wonderful friends and expert contacts have in turn reached out to their networks. And together, we offer the best wisdom in each of the categories that are changing in your life right now as you try to sort out what's what.

You will also read firsthand experiences of what it was personally like to go through the shock of being laid off. (Their names have been changed, but their words and stories are real.) Some readers will criticize this collection because each person's story ends on an up note. I chose these people on purpose. This book is not intended to be a "balanced exposé" on how horrible the economy is. You already know that. But what you might not know is that your own laid-off saga can also end on an up note. And my mission is to bring you proof that it's possible for you because it happened to them.

We are here for you within these pages. Here you will find the help, perspective, insights, and wisdom you need to take the next best steps in your life to keep moving forward toward your ultimate dreams.

And hope…here you will find the hope as well.

PART I

THE INNER GAME OF GETTING LAID OFF

CHAPTER 1

What to Expect When You're No Longer Expected

A high-speed car crash comes to mind just now. You have been barreling along at top speed for years. Working very long hours, even while in bumper-to-bumper traffic. Taking your PDA and laptop on vacations with you. Perhaps you've sacrificed a bit of your own health and peace of mind for the sake of the job and what it brings to you and your family. Things have been moving very fast, and you've been accelerating along with the world, pushing down on the accelerator to keep ahead of your competition and stay on the leading edge of your industry. There's something exhilarating about working at those outer reaches of your skills, your wits, your creativity, your ability to react, your capacity for excellence. You've been learning a lot about yourself and what you really can do. You've been able to give your spouse and children a life in a world that you never even knew existed when you were a kid.

But then it stops. With one visit from your manager, and maybe from someone in HR, you run head on into a wall. Done. Finito. Here's a box for your stuff. Ever so sorry. Sign this. Get out.

You've been laid off. And your career is the accordioned wreckage joining the heap of thousands of other careers piled up at this very same wall. Your job may have come to an unexpected, abrupt halt. But your heart and mind continue to surge forward at the same rate of speed as before, and you're in for some internal damage. No matter how well you thought you were buckled in, there's not a whole lot that can prepare your insides from the shock of the sudden, slamming stop.

Let's start with your head first. You may not have *loved* your job every single moment in the last year or so. And maybe lately it's gotten really unpleasant at work, especially with all those empty cubicles. Not to mention that idiot who has taken over your division without knowing anything about the business. But you relished the challenge still, and you had become attached to the habit of getting a paycheck every two weeks. Or you were proud to be associated with the prestige of the company name. Or you were five years away from retiring, and you're old enough to know how fast five years can go by. Or you were in the middle of a really great project that you loved. What's going to happen to that? That was your baby. Who's going to take care of it now? And shouldn't you have some input into who it gets handed off to? Uh. No. You no longer work there, remember? That project may or may not achieve its full potential. But no one is paying you to care about it anymore. In fact, with whatever severance payment you might have received, you're actually being paid not to care about it anymore. So you can just forget it. Right now.

And what about your overbooked calendar? That speech you were scheduled to give to the Western Region? That review committee status meeting that was to give you the go ahead to launch your pet project into Phase 6? All those lunch dates with clients who will show up on time, only to eat alone? Who cares? You don't have to anymore. Even when you wake up in the middle of the night with this vague, urgent feeling that you missed a meeting or forgot a crucial detail. That's just the phantom limb of your old identity wearing the memory of itself out. Go back to sleep. If you can.

So now let's move on to the matter of your heart. All those people you grew to care about. All that celebratory laughter over a project well done. All those ridiculous cakes, with everyone genuinely caring about each other's birthdays—turning the office into a jolly kindergarten room for just a few moments while the song is sung. That happiness survey you took every year. Wasn't there a question about whether you had a best friend at work? You had more than one best friend, you had a team of friends who were equally dedicated to the same level of passion and excellence you were (maybe some a little more, some a little less). All those people you personally mentored, groomed, and promoted. They were so grateful. They were also really great at volleyball, at the grill, at the holiday charity fundraising, at that Habitat for Humanity building project. So much fun.

Where are they now? At work. Where are you now? Not at work. What are they thinking about your sudden absence? That you're sick? That you got fired? That you got arrested? Isn't anyone going to call to make sure that you're okay? Maybe. Maybe not. It's not your job to worry about that either. And it's not their job to worry about you, especially when your empty desk might give them cause to worry about themselves.

A layoff hits everyone differently, of course, depending on their financial resources, self-esteem, support systems, networks, professional reputations, level of endurance, resilience, and optimism. But there do seem to be some common experiences that laid-off professionals report. You might like to know about them. At the very least, there's some comfort in knowing you're not alone.

Mixed Feelings

You're angry and glad at the same time. Maybe you've been worried about the prospect of getting laid off, and now you're relieved that the axe has finally fallen. Now you can replace that old worry of losing your job with the new worry of finding your next job. You're furious with your boss for not letting you know that this was around the corner—even that time when you explicitly asked. And you feel sorry for him, too, because you know his hands were tied. He had to drop the axe according to a management-enforced script; you know that. And it was killing him inside to do it. You know that, too. But still it was your neck, not his, which the axe dropped upon. And you're steamed. But then again…it must be really hard to be him right now.

Bewilderment

How could they let you go when there is so much dead weight still lying around the office? How could you have been so blind? Were you just lying to yourself when you thought that it couldn't happen to you? What were the signs that you missed? Could you possibly miss them again if this happens to you another time—assuming, that is, that you can even find a new job?

Crisis in Self-Worth

Will you be able to find a new job—especially in this economy? If so, when? If the company you worked so hard and successfully for could let you go so easily, would another company even recognize your abilities and appreciate you for what you have to offer? How can your family still respect you when you're not bringing in "your share" of the household income? What about all those sycophants who took your orders because you represented the next rung on their own career ladders? Would they even know you if you passed on the street?

Alienation

How could it possibly be that you haven't heard from *any* of your coworkers since you disappeared? They couldn't have forgotten you already, could they? Maybe they think you're a failure, and failure is catching, like in the Lyle Lovett song, when he sings, "Get it on your fingers and it crawls right up your sleeve." You're not contagious, everyone knows that. It's not rational to think that one person's failure might spread through the office like a flu bug. But sometimes humans aren't rational. Like your boss, when he laid you off.

Isolation

The cruel irony here is that just when you need most not to be alone, that's when you are. Everybody's at work. Your kids are at school. Your first days at home feel like the first few days at any new job: You hardly know what to do with yourself that contributes to anything in any kind of meaningful way. You don't know who you are in the context of this new identity. Nobody else does either, really, because they're waiting to take their cues from you. At least here you have the advantage of knowing where the coffeepot and the bathroom are.

Maybe you can go downtown. But the only people hanging out in the middle of the day at coffee shops are losers or "consultants." And we all know what that's code for, don't we?

Or you can go in with the morning rush. But then there's that possibility that you might make like Charlton Heston as Moses, pointing to the commuting crowd, and pronounce, "Beware! You could be next!" Oh. That would be crazy, wouldn't it? Better you should stay home, at least for a little while. At least until the shock wears off. But then, how long will that take?

Who are you now in this new phase of your life? Time *will* tell. And the good news is that, even though it doesn't seem so obvious or guaranteed right now, it's quite possible that you'll come out of this crisis the better for having gone through it. It's been known to happen. Lots of times. And there's no reason why yours can't be one of the happy-ending stories. It's not like the Good Luck Gate slammed shut a split second after you got laid off.

Your good fortune hasn't run out. Maybe it's just begun.

The best thing you can do:
Give yourself the chance to go through all the feelings that are coming your way.

The worst thing you can do:
Judge or rush yourself as you cycle through those feelings.

The first thing you should do:
Make a list of the things you can control positively and focus on that for now.

CHAPTER 2

New Career Realities and New Career Rules

When he was writing *Alice in Wonderland,* Lewis Carroll may have been writing for his time. But, in fact, he was writing for the ages. If there were ever a time when falling down the rabbit hole might actually feel *normal,* it's now. We're stuck in a universal fun house of distorting mirrors, advice from all corners that perhaps we would be better off not taking, narcissists telling us that black is white just because it is they who say so, political and business leaders pronouncing the world to be as they wish it were—not as it really is.

On the personal side, one day you're told not to worry about your job. The next day you're tossed out of it. Here. Drink me. And you'll grow to be oh so out of work. It's gotten so that you don't even want to commit to a lunch appointment next week with a client, much less plan your retirement.

How do you thrive under these conditions? Learn to love the paradox way. You might as well; you're stuck with it. And, paradoxically, once you find comfort in being somewhat out of control in an out-of-control world, you start to reclaim power over your life again.

Security is found in embracing insecurity. I expect you might hate hearing this. But we're actually lucky. Generations before us who have been thrown out of work were taken completely by surprise. The first rounds of layoffs in the modern industrial and post-industrial eras were catastrophic breaches of promise. Even if that promise was only a culturally implied one, it was still there. Our grandfathers and fathers dutifully marched out of their World War II and Korean War uniforms and into their civilian work clothes trusting that dedicated, high performance would net them security for the wife and kids, and a comfy (if not lavish) retirement on the back end. Even though their heads were filled with memories of the Great Depression and perhaps the firsthand horrors of war, there was one formula of stability that they could comfortably count on. Good work = good job = dependable income = kids get to go to college. And, at 65 or so, they got to retire to the golf course or La-Z-Boy.

They may not have realized it in the 1950s when they were putting in all that time at their labors, but their generation was destined to be the first wave of the demise of the job-for-life contract. Thousands upon thousands of dedicated, nose-to-grindstone employees of all socioeconomic levels had no idea that the pink slip was in their destiny. But it was. And then their retirement savings got sucker punched by Black Monday (October 19, 1987) when the Dow Jones Industrial Average dropped 22.6% in a single day.

We were young then, and maybe not paying so much attention. That was the business of grown-ups and, besides, it couldn't possibly happen again. Right? They'll fix it so it doesn't. That's what grown-ups do. I guess some things aren't fixable. Like economic cycles over time. And human nature.

So now we've come to this. And at least we can't say we had no warning. It's weirdly comforting just accepting that we are ensconced in what Wharton School of Business adjunct professor Greg Shea calls a *permanently roiling world,* what Peter Vaill, professor of management at Antioch University, calls *permanent white water.* We might as well learn to love it, because that's what we have from here on out. We can rage at the trends and swim against the current. But we'd just exhaust ourselves because the current is much stronger and more powerful than our puny little selves.

Or we can choose to accept the fact of our smallness in these times and learn how to work with the current to master the way our own lives flow.

You're a brilliant human being, blessed with talents, ideas, and creativity. There will never be another one like you ever again. You are also a unit of labor. I started really paying attention in college when during an English Lit class I first heard the William Blake expression *divine spark*. Coming from a high-drama family of ministers, composers, professors, reporters, authors, and spies, I came to believe that life would achieve its full potential—its rarified specialness—once I found my own divinely assigned spot on the soaring jet stream of purpose, effort, and ease.

I'm still romantic enough to believe that we all have our uniquely assigned position on that proverbial plane of flow and purpose. Some ideas you just can't grow out of. But time (and maybe a little maturity) has also shown me that my own divine spark works only when I connect it to others in a marketplace-meaningful way. And that makes me as ordinary and pedestrian as a mere cog in a machine.

And that has to be okay. We may be divinely sparked, but we're also cogs. And we have to take full responsibility to make sure we remain relevant and maintained and precision-tooled to serve the changing needs of our market. That means we can't be so romantic about who we are in the great cosmic scheme of things. Cogs are replaceable, and it's a bummer to think that maybe we are, too. But it's also liberating to know that there are specific things we can and should do to keep ourselves valuable in the changing market.

Says Shea, "How can we look at ourselves as units of labor without treating ourselves like pieces of meat? We need to be constantly asking ourselves what are the right skills we need to be developing, and what are the right experiences we need to be acquiring to stay current and relevant in a roiling marketplace. And we need to remember that we are uniquely dear souls. One of the many paradoxes of our time."

Be ready to show up; be ready to connect; be ready to be gone. Part of thriving in change, says Shea, is to be "increasingly dependent on intense and transient relationships. And that's a very weird place for human beings to be." In the past 20 years, we have become very fond of referring to work groups as teams. And a fact of team life is that players tend to change frequently, moving in and out of each others' lives—and back in again, months or even years later.

As a species, we're not too much different from all the other mammals in the animal kingdom. Regardless of whether we travel in packs or roam in solitude, we need the company of others, at least now and then. And we like to take our own time getting to know whether we can trust that stranger and showing the stranger that he or she can trust us. And once we've connected, it's our preference to disconnect only when it feels right and natural.

The work world has put a new timer on the developing of intimacies and trust. We're expected to show up and join up with teams of total strangers, spend more time with them than the ones we love, and then depart at the end of the day, or the end of the project, or the end of our useful service with barely a whimper. And that's just not natural.

No one's expecting you to love this new way. You don't even have to like it. But it's the way of things now, so don't just get used to it. Make it work for you. When you do, you'll discover that it will work for you in surprising ways. You may find that you're more comfortable, accepted, and forthcoming with a business colleague whom you have seen maybe twice in the past ten years than your own family members. You may speed up the career ladder—or lattice—much more quickly than you might have if you had stuck with the old-fashioned, slow-moving way of limited acquaintances and opportunities.

Additionally, transient relationships aren't necessarily temporary, fleeting, or even shallow. They can be deeply rewarding, endlessly giving, hugely helpful, and lavishly networking. They can also be people whom you've never met in person at all, but you consider them to be among your closest friends. They are extremely utilitarian when you need them the most for specific purposes. And these distant relationships don't mind being called out of the blue, just as you don't mind. It's the way of doing things.

The "Bowling Alone" researchers may lament the demise of the old, intimate, small-town network that characterized American life of 40 years ago. But in its place, whole new networks have sprung up in which we can call toll-free to Europe, reach out to India for a friendly, familiar voice and some technical assistance on our website, or ask a friend of a friend of a friend if he or she wouldn't mind helping you with an important project. And unlike 40 years ago, we're more likely to hear the word *yes* from that friend of a friend of a friend...even if that person is half a world away.

To thrive in this new way, we have to learn to love the word *gone*. This latticed network of wonderful connections doesn't work unless we're prepared to leave it or let someone else in the network go. Or let our job go, and along with it our sense of security. Because, if you think of it, security—at least the security we can reach for outside of ourselves—has always been just an illusion anyway.

Prepare for success by training for disaster. In Shea's book, *Your Job Survival Guide,* he compares navigating one's career life with kayaking. One of the first skills that kayakers learn is the "Eskimo roll," in which paddlers can easily bring themselves back upright out of the water, should they tip over. It's a fluid movement, so to speak, and it actually looks like a lot of fun to do. But it's also an essential skill because kayakers could face drowning should they not be able to maneuver a full 360 degrees to get their faces back out of the water.

This skill is an important part of the kayaker's toolkit. And learning to do it smoothly and certainly is their ticket to being able to enjoy the rest of the sport. Kayakers accept tipping over as an integral part of the experience of kayaking. And they don't beat themselves up for "failing" to stay upright. They just train themselves to smoothly bring themselves right again and then get on with things.

There is nothing comfortable or guaranteed about your career life. If you've picked this book up after having been laid off, you already know that only too well. Your greatest security is letting go of the need for certainty, learning to enjoy the ride, and preparing to get a dunking now and then. Just remember that you'll reach your goals faster and have a better time doing it when you build your networks and take care of your friends along the way. Even the ones you haven't met yet.

The best thing you can do:
Assume success.

The worst thing you can do:
Panic and shut your mind down to opportunities and ideas.

The first thing you should do:
Something for yourself, ideally in the company of someone you care about...and who cares about you.

CHAPTER 3

You're Still in Control

You've probably noticed that there's little rhyme or reason in this new era of layoffs. First of all, it seems to have come out of nowhere. (It wasn't that long ago when employers were talking about the War for Talent and how essential it is to find and keep great people. Not to mention the upcoming labor shortage where there aren't enough people to replace the retiring Baby Boomers.)

Second, it seems as though stellar performance ratings won't secure your job. It might not net you more than merely an *extra* sincere, "Gosh, we're really sorry." And, perhaps, a long tenure at the company might make you eligible for *two* boxes for your desk stuff rather than just one. If the company is determined to cut head count by a certain percentage, no amount of exposure, of reminding the boss how successful you've been in helping the company achieve its goals, will save your job. They'll miss you when you've gone, but they've already determined that you're gone anyway.

Where do you find control in this mess? From within. You're still in charge.

You control who owns your career. If you're mainly worried about "recession-proofing your job," you don't own your career. When you're worried about keeping your job, you have given ownership of your career over to your employer—who just may not want it anymore, regardless of how well you play internal politics. This position is keeping you rigidly attached to the perception of security. Real security can be found when you regard your job as only a small moment in your career. Control is yours when you take on a lifetime perspective of rolling over times of plenty and times of not-so-much, with you always at the helm, shifting your weight and course-correcting as external circumstances change.

You control your status as an "A" player. Notice I didn't say employee-of-choice. This is about you in the context of your life, not in the context of whom you might work for. You never have to lose your faith in your ability to provide top-notch services and thought leadership. You don't need a business card with someone else's logo to claim your own knowledge, skills, and abilities to make a meaningful difference.

You control your identity. It's time to define yourself by what impassions you, not by who employs you. Who are you really? To borrow from that old cliché, when you're on your deathbed what will you be *glad* you had spent more time doing? Think about how you would proudly complete this sentence: "I'm the person my friends can always count on to _____."
Any job title (IT specialist, program manager, vice president) can't grammatically complete that sentence. Plus, I would bet that the services promised by those labels wouldn't qualify for the emotional buzz you would get by identifying those activities and characteristics that really do represent who you are—especially to the people who love you. Your identity sums up how you make the world a better place. Sometimes your job makes it easier for you to do that. Sometimes it doesn't. Your identity is expressed by your values, life's purpose, and the activities you do to support those things. Not the title on your business card.

You control your self-worth. Your identity and self-worth are much more interwoven with each other than they are with any job you could possibly have. Many people are able to make a career out of the values and missions that ignite their personal passion. Lucky them. But even when those jobs go away, that doesn't mean that their self-respect necessarily plummets. Although it feels great to work at your full potential doing things that matter to you, your job status should *not* affect your self-esteem. You have control over how you regard the face you see in the mirror, independent of who thinks you're a keeper in the company and who doesn't.

You control how you manage your resources. When you see *resources,* you might first think *money.* And that's part of it. Making and saving money are certainly hot topics these days. But resources also include your relationships, your reputation in your community and among your professional colleagues, your openness to making new friends, your receptivity to creative ideas and brainstorming, even your own willingness to shift your identity and tell a different (and truer) story about who you are and what you have to offer. All these things are your personal resources, and you can use them as valuable tools to build a future that makes the best use of your potential.

You control how you interpret these times of uncertainty. True, these times represent a catastrophe to many, but do they have to be a catastrophe to *you?* They don't have to. They could, if you focus on lamenting the structure and familiarity that you stand to lose as your company downsizes. Or if you shift your perspective and ask yourself possibility-oriented questions, these times could represent new opportunities for growth, taking on new skills that will serve you well into the future, making new friends, and building new business relationships. When you look back on this time, you may discover that this was the era when you discovered whole new wells of resources and talents you had no idea existed within you.

You have control over what lessons this time will teach your family for generations to come. If you're a parent, you know that one of your more important life assignments is teaching your children how to find a place for themselves in the world. You can teach your children to relate to the world as a basically hostile place filled with uncertainty and pain. Or you can teach your children that the world is basically a friendly place filled with uncertainty and opportunities. You don't have to completely hide from them the fact that you don't know exactly how this time will play out. But you can also model a fundamental faith that no matter what happens, everyone will be okay. The future stories that you make now through your actions and behaviors could serve to inspire many generations in the future when they face their own uncertain times.

The best thing you can do:
Recognize that this period of layoffs—whether it actually happens to you—is just another moment in time, having nothing to do with your essential value and meaning.

The worst thing you can do:
Accept this less-abundant time as rock-solid proof that efforts are futile and the world is a hostile, unwelcoming environment for the likes of you.

The first thing you should do:
Hug someone you love and count your blessings.

PART II

PREPARING FOR A LAYOFF

CHAPTER 4

Are You on the Layoff List?

So many people report that being laid off came as a total surprise. One morning they show up for work as usual. An hour later they're sitting behind their steering wheel stunned, with a box of pictures and books in the backseat.

It's bad enough to lose your job. But to have it take you by surprise is just unfathomable. How can you read the tea leaves on something like this so that it doesn't happen to you? Or so that it doesn't happen to you again?

Here are some signs that you might be on a list of people to be laid off:

- Your company has hit hard times and has publicly announced that it will institute "cost-cutting measures."
- Your industry sector has taken a dive on Wall Street.
- Your company has been acquired, and there's someone just like you already ensconced in the acquiring company.
- Your company just bought your competitor, and there's someone just like you in the newly acquired company.
- You work for a closely held family business—and you're not family.
- You work for a publicly traded business that prides itself on being "one big happy family."
- You've been asked to research ways the business can reduce expenses.
- Your otherwise congenial boss starts avoiding you.
- Your otherwise congenial boss starts snapping at you.
- Your boss starts looking at you strangely.
- Your boss starts looking right through you.

- You inexplicably feel compelled to ask your boss if there's about to be a layoff.
- You are one of the highest paid people in the organization.
- You are one of the lowest paid people in the organization.
- You're somewhere in the middle.
- You wonder how your long-time coworker could be taking such a lengthy leave of absence without saying good-bye.
- There is an unusually bulky FedEx package from headquarters that's addressed to your local HR department.
- There is absolutely nothing out of the ordinary going on in the company whatsoever.
- You picked this book up just out of curiosity.
- You have a job.

The best thing you can do:
Recognize that everyone is subject to being laid off.

The worst thing you can do:
Think it won't happen to you.

The first thing you should do:
Keep in mind that getting laid off has nothing to do with your performance.

Voice of Experience: Rob

As a company, we had already gone through a challenging time in 2000, and my company was one of the few in Silicon Valley that didn't lay off anyone. In fact, we became famous for the way we all pitched in to save everyone's jobs. I took a 6% hit to my salary that year and took a lot of vacation time. Everyone was doing it, and morale was really high.

Even after that crisis was over, though, the sales force—where I worked—still went through many changes and restructurings, which I think were detrimental to the business. The focus shifted to what particular people were doing rather than the greater good of the company. So, when I was relocated from headquarters in San Jose to Colorado, the thought did cross my mind that being so far away from headquarters might put me at a greater risk for being laid off.

I was in Colorado two and a half years when my boss called me over a weekend and said that the sales force had been restructured again. And he had good news and bad news. The good news was that I still had a job. The bad news was that he was no longer my boss. My new manager was a guy in Los Angeles now, a coworker and someone I'd worked with for over ten years.

I figured that if you were going to cut people, you'd do that during the restructure. So I thought, "Well, I didn't get cut, so I guess I'm safe."

Two months later my boss said, "I need you to come to a 7:30 a.m. meeting. Can you be there?" I knew this was the big day they were going to let people go. And I thought he was asking me to come in early to stand in for him at some other meetings while he was laying people off. When I walked in, he met me in the lobby and said, "I'm not allowed to say more than a couple of words to you. I have to let you go."

Within an hour I had gotten my personal files off my laptop and my things out of my cube. I was walked out like a criminal. And that was the end of my 15 plus years with my company. I couldn't even say good-bye to friends and colleagues I had known for 15 years.

I was in shock, but I was relieved at the same time. I could stop all this speculating with every reorg, and I didn't have to look over my shoulder anymore. Then panic set in. We immediately put our house on the market. And I spent the next month fixing it up, landscaping, tiling a bathroom, and painting the whole house. The smell of anxiety is the smell of latex paint.

My wife and I bickered a lot during that first month. And the kids knew that "Daddy lost his job." But we also worked very hard to reassure them that even though we didn't know what was going to happen and that we might have to move, everything would be okay. The house didn't sell.

The day I got laid off I did my resumé, having to build it from the ground up. I also sent emails to customers and friends I'd worked with, letting them know I appreciated working with them all those years, and that felt good.

I immediately started letting people know I was looking for a new job. Networking is huge. My wife even talked to parents at my children's school. And it's amazing how quickly people mobilize. I started interviewing within a month and a half, and within three months I found work, which is pretty amazing when you think about the fact that at that time the big high-tech companies in Colorado were laying off people.

At first I was worried that being laid off would be a problem for me, that people would assume that I had been a poor performer. But this is so commonplace now, people aren't jumping to that conclusion.

The good that came out of this whole experience is the reminder of how important your network is. Contacts are so important, and I had taken them for granted. Every interview I had was because someone recommended me. And I wasn't the ideal candidate for the job that I'm in now, but someone personally vouched for me.

On the flip side, I must have sent out 100 resumés and wasted about two weeks going on websites and filling out those stupid online forms. I did not get one callback. Not one.

The best thing you can do:

Keep your network active, no matter how comfortable you feel at your present job.

The worst thing you can do:

Waste your time with online applications. If you see that a company has an opening that interests you, use your network to connect with someone inside the company you can meet directly.

The first thing you should do:

Immediately get the word out that you're in the market for a job. Don't let the shame or negative self-talk stop you.

CHAPTER 5

Financial: What to Do Before You Get Laid Off

Even if you aren't facing an immediate possibility of a layoff, there are actions you can and should take now to put yourself in the best possible financial position to absorb the shock should the time come. This advice comes from Mark Gibbs, Atlanta-based CPA and certified financial planner, who says that being employed will make it easier for you to make some of these changes. So consider doing them now.

Acquire a home equity loan. Because lending institutions may be more stringent with mortgages now, you stand a better chance of qualifying for a HELOC (and at better terms) if you're employed. Their new stringency will help protect you from taking on more debt than the house is worth. And the interest rates are certainly much lower than credit card rates. "Use your HELOC only as a last resort, of course," says Gibbs, "but make sure it's in place so it's there if you should ever need it."

Move your savings to an online savings account. Compare interest rates between the brick-and-mortar banks in your neighborhood and those that are available via online financial institutions. If the trends continue to hold steady, you are most likely to discover that online interest rates are much better than what you can get in a conventional bank. The process of moving funds from your conventional accounts to online accounts is smooth and easy. Make sure the online institution is guaranteed by the FDIC, so that your deposits are just as secure as they are in a conventional bank (up to $250,000 as of this writing).

Get a term life insurance policy separate from your employer-provided policy. Remember that your employer-provided policy probably expires upon your termination. So one day you and your family may be covered, and the next day you aren't. When you're reeling from the shock of being laid off, you might not be thinking of these details of your financial life. So think about them now when you're calm. As an individual insurance holder, you may get better terms than the terms of the group policy your employer has, anyway. So consider your individual policy as your primary life insurance policy, and the company coverage as "gravy," says Gibbs.

Get a thorough physical now and fix your health problems while you're covered under your employer's plan. Your employer-provided health coverage (which will continue to be available to you for 18 months under COBRA,* if you decided to take advantage of it) is probably more expensive than anything you would be willing to pay for on your own, especially in a crisis mode that might be around the corner—but it's probably also more valuable. A complete physical now, along with pricey tests, such as colonoscopies, will reveal conditions that you can take care of right away. Or in an even happier scenario, you'll get a clean and current bill of health that you can then present to your new health insurance provider, should you need to get your own insurance. Then you can qualify for better and cheaper insurance and agree to high deductibles with the confidence that you probably won't be needing serious medical treatment while you're in the market for a new job.

Stockpile your cash. Gibbs recommends that you take such steps as selling your unwanted clutter on eBay or Craig's List;

---

* You may decide very early to forgo your COBRA coverage and find alternative health insurance. However, even if you decide not to take advantage of it now, you can change your mind within 60 days of leaving your last job, says Gibbs. Which could come in very handy should bad luck come in twos. "If you get injured or require other medical care during that 60-day period, you can retroactively enroll in COBRA and receive coverage." Keep in mind, however, that you'll have to pay those back premiums retroactively as well.

reduce your 401(k) contributions—just for now—and put that cash into savings, pay only the minimums on your credit card balances—again, just for now. Stop carrying credit cards entirely, of course.

Level with the kids. Let them know that everyone will be cutting back and you are counting on their cooperation. Reassure them that while it's your job to be in charge of the family's money issues, they can do their part by turning things off and coming up with ideas about how to save money wherever they can. This is also the time to tell them that nonnecessities are out of the question—at least for a little while. So please don't ask for things when "no" is the most likely answer. That just makes it harder on you.

Level with your former spouse, if you have a good relationship. Depending on your relationship and your legal agreements, you may find that it's better to approach your former spouse directly to ask for some creative approach to your financial arrangements. If you're the one on the hook for child support payments, the courts aren't likely to let you ease off that responsibility. Do what's legally proper and morally right in your responsibilities as a parent, of course. But now is an excellent time to brainstorm with your children's other parent to see how creative solutions can help everyone get through this pinched time.

Break your habits. Sugar, alcohol, tobacco, caffeine, happy hour, pay-per-view, comfort shopping. You've been meaning to cut back on those things for a while now. No time like the present. Presents, too, by the way.

Don't kill time at stores. Take a walk instead. Or go to the library. Or read in the car. Stores are in the business of putting desires in your head and products in your basket. You're in the family business of putting money in your accounts. And keeping it there.

Gibbs, as well as any financial advisor you would speak to, recommends that every household have an emergency fund of at least three to six months of expenses. If you've been in the habit of living paycheck to paycheck, it's a little late to be beating yourself up about not having socked away money over the past years of plenty. That was then, now is now. Get in the habit of keeping your cash now, no matter what your immediate employment situation is. And you will be better positioned for absorbing the shock of a layoff, should it be in your immediate future.

The best thing you can do:
Think ahead and make easy but valuable changes in your financial life.

The worst thing you can do:
Assume it's too late to change your financial ways.

The first thing you should do:
Remind yourself that most of the changes you will make are excellent money management habits during any economic period.

CHAPTER 6

Set the Tone for How You Leave

You haven't been laid off yet, but the handwriting is definitely on the wall. Your department has been reduced one person at a time for weeks now; all those empty cubicles are reminders that you could be next. There's a room down the hall where behind the closed door your coworkers are transformed from confident people with jobs to stunned people without jobs. You know you're destined to take that walk down the hall. It's just a matter of time.

This may feel as though your career is coming to an end, but it's important to remember that it's only this one particular job that is closing down. Says Libby Gill, a Los Angeles-based executive coach who specializes in helping people in transition (as well as a former entertainment industry executive who has had to lay off people), this is not the *end* of your career—it's a *moment* in your career. And how you handle the layoff experience could make a huge difference to both your long-term future and your immediate prospects. She says that there are three distinct tasks ahead of you.

Accept the News Gracefully

Jobs may be short-lived. But careers are longer-lasting. And reputations will follow you forever. So, however much you want to scream, blame, or use words that would embarrass your mother, do yourself a favor and make it easy on these people to break the hard news to you. (If you're in complete charge of your emotions, you could actually muster up some pity for these people. They might be in the same boat you are, only they don't know it yet. It's not unheard of for the head of a department—after laying off the entire team—to be told, "There's one more package for you to do.")

However you react, just remember that this is just another short day in your long career, and you will be seeing these people in years to come in different companies, industry conferences, and so on. They may be your executioners today, but in a year from now, they could be your clients. Or they could be applicants to a job that you have posted now that you're securely settled in your next, better job. No matter how you will meet these people again, the chances are excellent that A) you will, and B) you will be really glad you didn't behave in a cringe-making way.

"Be as dignified as you can because then you'll be able to look back and be proud of yourself," says Gill. "You'll be able to retain your self-respect well into the future. And these people will always remember your ability to handle a terribly tough personal moment with grace and propriety."

Tears, shock, and sadness are all natural reactions, says Gill, and they are okay to show in such a horrible meeting. But lashing out in a personally insulting or an out-of-control way will make enemies of the very people you will want to have in your corner as you move forward in your career.

Mourn Authentically
Even though you should *control* your emotions, no one is expecting you to *deny* your emotions—even the extreme ones that can best be expressed using four-letter words. If you've been passionate about your work up to this point, and successful, the chances are excellent that there's a huge piece of your self-esteem and identity wrapped up in that job you just lost. And that just has to hurt. There's no amount of professionalism that you can call up that will excuse you completely from feeling the wrenching loss.

"Deal with your pain privately and in the company of your most supportive friends and family members," says Gill. "Do what you need to do to get the rage out of your system. Write an angry, venomous letter to your boss—but don't send it, of course. Howl at the moon, if you have to. Break something (making sure it's something that's cheap and meaningless to you). Vent to your friends—especially the ones who don't mind sitting with you as you work the same story over and over and over again."

Give yourself the time and chance to fully feel the shock and the pain of the layoff. Do it in a safe place among people who will patiently support you as you work to get the steam out of your system. And then get on with your life.

Regroup Strategically

Even as you're mourning authentically, you will soon feel that you're ready to take up the business of your future again. And when you're ready to take this step, you will start to feel much better. Gill recommends that within a few days or a week after you've been laid off that you contact your boss and request an "exit interview" to review some of the details that you might not have heard during the meeting while your head was buzzing.

"You're on your game now, your most positive, your most collected," she says. "This is the time to review the details of your severance package and all the benefits that might be due you, including vacation time, retraining, outplacement counseling. If it's only been a day or two since you were laid off, you might also want to talk about how the news will be communicated internally and externally. If you have a chance to control the way your termination is worded, take it! It could set the tone for your new job search in a very positive way."

Gill also recommends that you write a positive letter about your experiences in the company, what you've learned and your appreciation for the experiences and friends you made during your tenure there. Send that letter to the CEO, cc'ing your immediate supervisor, the head of your department, and the HR department.

And start requesting letters of your own. Ask your boss for a letter of recommendation, and reach out to all the immediate connections that you have within the company for letters and the promise of a positive referral. (Gill says you should also be prepared to write those letters yourself, and send them drafts for their editing and signature. That's actually a good thing, she says, because you're making it easier on people who are already feeling awkward, guilty, and maybe a little overwhelmed by all the extra work they've had to take on as the company continues to downsize. Additionally, you can control what is being said and how your strengths and gifts are positioned. Make sure they know that this is just a draft for their consideration, and that they're free to edit the material to best match their voice and opinions.)

"It's great to have these letters completed while your connections are fresh and sympathy for you is high," she says. "You'll probably find that more often than not your former coworkers will be thrilled to have the chance to help you find your next job. They were your work friends before, and your getting laid off hasn't changed that. Plus, some of them are probably thinking that maybe you'll help pave the way for them to move on to their next jobs as well."

By the way...about those former coworkers: Why don't they call? You're the one whose world has been rocked. You're the one who is grieving. You're the one who's bereft. So, it just follows that you're the one whose phone should be ringing off the proverbial hook. Your living room should be filled with flowers. Your mailbox stuffed with cards. Your email inbox (which is now embarrassingly dot yahoo, dot gmail, dot aol, or dot hotmail, instead of dot big, fancy, high-prestige company) should be stuffed with introductions to potential new employers. You shouldn't be able to close your refrigerator door with all the casseroles in there just waiting for you to emerge from your stupor, stagger from couch to microwave, and barely bring yourself to program a quick reheat.

But noooooo. Nothing. You could be abducted by aliens for all they would ever know. Or care.

This is where human nature trumps Emily Post. Your former coworkers just don't have a clue what to say to you. They feel terrible about what happened to you, and wonder if it might happen to them. And then they feel terrible that they're thinking about themselves when it really did already happen to you. And so they wait until the right thing to say comes to them. But then it never really does. And the longer they wait, they know, the worse it's going to be. Then, what do you know? Months have just flown right by. Surely they couldn't reach out to you now. What could they possibly say to earn your forgiveness and understanding?

Gill says that it's really up to you to be the bigger and better person and reach out to them first. Put on your authentic, positive, grounded happy voice and call them to tell them how much you've enjoyed working with them, "Yeah, it's a bummer what happened, but you know what? Good things will come of this." Tell *them* it was an honor to work with them. Tell *them* how much you enjoy their friendship. Tell *them* that in a month or so you'd love to get together with them for lunch or something. And put it in your calendar to make that date.

You might not have any control over the fact that you're no longer with the company. But you have every bit of control over the tone that you leave on. Depart on a high note, with head held high, and your network of supporters—both inside and outside the company—will be so glad to be on your team as you search for your next opportunity.

The best thing you can do:
Maintain your dignity so that you can keep your self-respect.

The worst thing you can do:
Lose your composure out of fear or anger.

The first thing you should do:
Think of your friends as your support squad and remember that they want to help you. Even if they don't quite know how.

CHAPTER 7

Plan Your Exit

Do you remember that weird workplace television show with Calista Flockhart, *Ally McBeal?* Two details stick in my mind about that show: the unisex office bathroom (thank heavens that was a trend that never caught on), and some advice the main character received as a method to bolster her confidence and motivation. "Give yourself a soundtrack." You might have scoffed at that idea when you saw the show. But now that you're walking down the hall to what might be the last meeting of your tenure at your company, a soundtrack is beginning to sound like a good idea. What will it be? The Pointer Sisters' song "I'm So Excited"? Richard Wagner's "The Ride of the Valkyries"? "Don't Worry Be Happy" by Bobby McFerrin? Personally, for me it would be a toss-up between "Got My Own Thing Now" and "Do It This Way" by the Squirrel Nut Zippers. (I might even strut down the hall like I would in a New Orleans jazz funeral, parasol and all. That could be cool. It would certainly leave a story behind. On second thought, no. Don't do it. You'd get fired before you got laid off.) Whatever song you choose, make sure it's not Roy Orbison's "Crying."

Almost every unexpectedly concluding job commences the shutdown process with a long walk by you down a hall to a room with a closed door. You pretty much know who's behind that door—your boss and maybe someone from HR. You know you want to handle the meeting with as much dignity as possible, but you're afraid you're going to lose it. In fact, just thinking about the possibility that you might lose it takes you that much closer to actually showing more emotion than you'd prefer. It's going to hurt. You just know that going in.

That walk from your desk to that door is your last chance to regroup and prepare. If you don't have a theme song already queued up on your emotional iPod, Libby Gill has some suggestions on how you can square your shoulders, lift your chin, and call up your inner hero—or jazzman—for that hard moment when you hear the inevitable words.

Remember what's important to you. Yes, your immediate livelihood is important. But there are bigger things in life that are even more important: your family, your lifelong career, your reputation, your chances of landing a terrific new job. You need these people who are about to lay you off in your corner. You need great letters of recommendation from them. When you remember what's really important to you, you'll summon your dignity and professionalism that will keep this last meeting as stately as possible. You won't be the only person in the room who will exhale relief.

Have a mantra. Chants didn't just start in the modern, woo-woo New Age era. Humanity has known them to work since the beginning of time. Find one short word or a quick phrase that you can focus on, such as *my family comes first* or *I'm okay*. And repeat that message all the way down the hall—preferably silently. By the time you take your seat, you may not be okay, but at least you'll be calm. And you might even notice how weird it is that that mundane expression *have a seat* may be the last order you take from your boss. (Ironically, it was probably also the first instruction you followed when you were interviewing for that job you're about to lose. Amazing how three little words can bookend a job so tidily.)

Go in knowing that you are okay for now. Whether you have three months' or six months' expenses socked away, or whether you just have enough to last you through your severance package, you are okay *right now*. You can return to thinking about your personal money issues in the privacy of your own car. Don't start doing it now.

Go to your happy place. This might sound silly, but doing whatever you need to do to keep your composure is imperative, even if it means resorting to everything short of bringing in a security blanket. No one needs to know what's going on in your mind that lends you a serene, relaxed, even somewhat detached demeanor as you're listening to the company's plans to systematically dismantle your world. Call up the memory of that time on the beach on Maui. Or the smell of sunblock by the sea at Rehoboth, or the satisfying way your goggles clung to your face at the top of that ski trail at Squaw Valley, or the homey, familiar smell of your child's canister of Play-Doh. Or chocolate chip cookies. Or even just the vanilla. Or the texture of margarita salt on the tip of your tongue. Something in your buzzing brain is bound to comfort you if you find it and lasso it in.

Life is still full of sensory memories of great stuff. Now is the perfect time to put them to good use. Even if it's only in your mind.

Oh. So you blew it? You can still clean up the mess. Okay, so you've just discovered something about yourself. You don't have superhuman control over your emotions after all. And something popped out of your head, heart, and then your mouth before you had the chance to zip it.

So now, on top of the devastation to discover you have been laid off through no fault of your own, *you owe an apology to the very people who took your job away!* Could anything be more unjust in this world? Most certainly. But right now it doesn't feel like it.

Gill says that before you do anything else, calm down and try to objectively assess that memory that's making you cringe. Was it really all that bad? Or are you just feeling super-sensitive right now? Crying isn't bad. Asking why isn't bad. Going into what Oprah Winfrey calls "the ugly cry" and wailing "whyyyyyy" like you're Lucille Ball...that might be a memory you'll wish you could rewind and then erase. Too late. It's done. Still, no big deal. You're only human, after all.

It's when you have discovered to your cringing toes-deep regret that you called your boss a name that consisted of only four letters or reminded her of a certain moment at a party a couple of years ago (remember? That was the moment you promised her you'd tell no one) that might require some cleaning up on your part. Ugh. How do you apologize for the absolutely unforgiveable? You just do, that's all.

Gill says that when you apologize, cop to the thing that makes you cringe the most. Start with, "Oh my gosh, I was such a jerk, I can't believe I said that. I sure hope you can find a way to accept my apology."

It might be difficult, and it might even feel pointless—you've lost your job anyway, what good will an apology do? Even if your totally over-the-top behavior didn't negatively affect your termination terms, apologizing is simply the right thing to do. Plus, says Gill, it's good for you.

"There's something really powerful in taking responsibility for being wrong," she says. "Your apology may not be accepted. Your former boss may not want to give you the chance to express your remorse. Your colleagues might turn their backs on you. But at least you know in your heart that you tried to do the right thing. You will have more confidence when you have to reenter that group in the future—like an industry conference. You will at least know that you did all you could."

Once you've done the apologizing you need to do, Gill says there's one more step in the clean-up process: Move on.

"You've assessed it, you've cleaned it up as best you can, and now you've got to move forward," she says. "Otherwise, you're just giving yourself one more excuse to beat yourself up and hold yourself back. You can't do that because now's the time [for] you to stay strong, focused, and back in control so you can find your next job."

The best thing you can do:
Remember you're only human.

The worst thing you can do:
Stress yourself out so much that you lose control.

The first thing you should do:
Remember you're only human!

Voice of Experience: Caroline

The company I worked for was so large that there was always a reorg happening somewhere. But I was a top performer in the company, getting a bonus every year, even in those years when they weren't giving out bonuses. So reorgs never bothered me. In fact, I was on a lot of the strategy teams.

The Monday it happened, I got a message to attend a mandatory 10 a.m. meeting. Because I knew it was the day of layoffs, I knew exactly what that meeting meant. In this company, when you get laid off, you just disappear. And they let the survivors just figure it out. But I had very strong loyalties with the people I'd worked with. So before I went into the meeting, I called a few of the people I worked most closely with to let them know what was probably going to happen.

It's funny the things that go through your head. I was really happy I was dressed nicely. I could go out looking classy. I had just decided I was going to get out the door, head held high, and not cry until I left this office.

I couldn't even talk to my partner about it that night. The next morning and afternoon, a few people called me from the office to tell me they were stunned, worried about me, and wanted to be my advocate inside. That day, I was really grateful to them for doing that. But the next day I was thinking, "Why would I want to go back to a company that doesn't want me?" I worked my tail off for this company; how could they not value me?

I felt genuinely betrayed by one particular person. In addition to being a coworker of mine, we are friends. And he knew on Friday. I had left him a voicemail message over the weekend about something work related. But he didn't get back to me, which was strange. I realized later he didn't call me back because he didn't want to tell me, or not tell me. Even though I understand he could not have told me and keep his job, it has fundamentally changed my view of that person.

Before, I would have trusted anything that person told me as gospel. Now I'd think, "Grain of salt." This experience changed my view of work and what work relationships are and what appropriate weight to give them.

My boyfriend and I had planned a trip to Europe, and because it was already paid for, we decided to go anyway. Sitting in my house was not going to help, or bring the money back. I was on the coast of Scotland one day and stepped into a cybercafé to email my parents. An email was waiting for me asking whether I was willing to come back. It was actually a promotion into a role that's more suitable to where I want my career to go long term.

I looked at the new role and realized that I really could contribute to what these people are doing. So, it was easy to let go of my resentment.

That turned out to be one of the best vacations of my adult life. Probably because I was in denial during the first half of the trip. And I was so relieved during the second half that we could have been touring the sewage-treatment plants of Europe and I would have been totally happy.

I'm back, sitting at my original desk, with the same phone number and the same view outside my window. The only thing that has really changed is me.

The best thing you can do:
Think about where it is you want to go. And make your choices accordingly.

The worst thing you can do:
Burn your bridges on your way out. One of the guys who got laid off when I did was obviously angry. And I remember thinking: "Thank you for saying all the things that are in my head. But I'm so glad they're not coming out of my mouth."

The first thing you should do:
Take a ruthless look at your finances. Find fat that you can trim. A big step to taking control of your life is just understanding your financial situation.

PART III

KNOW YOUR RIGHTS

CHAPTER 8

What You Can Expect from a Severance Package

Unfortunately, the answer can be summed up in two words: *Absolutely nothing.* Which isn't to say that you won't receive some kind of severance offer. But unless a formal severance plan is part of the company's published policy (and that policy is up-to-date), or unless a severance package is a part of your own individual employment contract, your company can decide what it wants to offer you and what it wants from you in return. You can always say no, of course, or perhaps submit a counter offer. But the terms are very much at the company's sole discretion, at least at the outset.

There are, however, certain provisions that are commonly found in severance packages. And they reflect those things that a company's management is most worried about. Remember, if you're on the loose out there in the big, wide world, you could be a liability to its reputation as a good provider of quality products and services and an excellent employer. Companies know that their reputation is golden, and they're willing to part with a certain amount of their gold to make sure that it remains intact.

Says attorney Barbara Johnson, partner in the Washington, DC office of Paul, Hastings, Janofsky & Walker, "The key thing is to remember that companies are looking for as broad and as extensive a release as state law will allow. They want to take as much latitude as they have to make sure that they won't end up in protracted litigation with an employee whom they've paid money to."

So here's what you might see in your severance package:

- A statement of your departure date
- Some kind of financial arrangement, whether it is in a lump sum or paid out over certain number of months
- An agreement that you won't say anything disparaging about the company, what it does or how it treats its employees
- A reassurance from you that you won't try to take its remaining employees or customers
- A no-return agreement that says you will not apply for another job at the same company
- A promise from you that you will be cooperative should there be an investigation in the future

Johnson, whose practice represents employers, advises that you can try to negotiate a custom package if you think it's worth the time and effort. But remember, if you're one of thousands of people who are being laid off by your company, your organization has already invested a lot of time and money developing a severance agreement that meets the company's needs and reflects what it's prepared to do for you.

The best thing you can do:
Don't take it personally, especially in situations of mass layoffs.

The worst thing you can do:
Get embroiled in the woulda, coulda, shouldas so much that you're not able to move forward with your life.

The first thing you should do:
Take your time to read and fully understand the severance contract that's been presented to you.

CHAPTER 9

Stop! Just Say No

Before you sign a thing...*don't sign a thing!* For so many people, it takes more time to buy a car (all day long) than it does to lose a job during a layoff. (One stroke of the pen and you're gone.) Too bad it's not reversed. But the stress, shock, and pressure to either not make a scene, be cooperative, leave with dignity, or just get your belongings and get home only make it easy on the people who want to dismiss you. Doesn't do you any good at all.

In fact, your being super-cooperative by signing that severance package right then and there could cost you many thousands of dollars. And you have every right and reason to hold off. Now that you know this, recognize any pressure or implied threat as Corporate's need to move things along. You're probably not the only layoff they're doing this round, and they have papers to process. So, don't waste your time or their time with chitchat and a showy display of deliberation (that would be agonizing for you, too). But don't give into any pressure to take that conveniently offered pen and put it to paper. You haven't signed anything in the throes of shock, confusion, and upset in the past. Why do it now? Just because they told you to?

What are they going to do if you don't? Fire you?

Take it easy (especially right now, while your head is spinning). And take your time. Alan L. Sklover, a New York-based attorney specializing in employee rights, says that you have three jobs when you think you're about to be terminated (and signing the severance package immediately isn't one of them. In fact, not signing it is).

Show No Emotion

Now is the time for the mother of all game faces. You may be feeling all the anger, shock, betrayal, resentment, and unfairness that go along with being a high performer who has just been given the boot, but don't show it. By giving in to your emotions, there's no telling what you might say. But management is much calmer than you are right now, and they've been trained to pay attention to how you behave.

"If you misbehave, act in anger, or strike out in any way, that's good enough reason for them to terminate you right then and there," says Sklover. "I've known circumstances where loud voices have been termed *workplace violence.* Then they have good reason to terminate you, without a severance package."

Gather Data

Another reason to keep your cool is to keep your head clear so that you can pay very close attention to what's being said to you. Take notes, ask questions, and listen very carefully. This termination team may have a script that they must adhere to—otherwise their own attorneys wouldn't be able to sleep at night—but asking them questions forces them to go off script, and you never know what might pop out of their mouths. Sklover says that he's heard of circumstances when someone on the termination team said, "You were about to retire soon, anyway, weren't you?" or "What are you worried about? Your husband makes plenty of money." You probably don't need to be reminded to take notes—even with a shaking hand—do you?

Make No Commitments

Thanks to the Older Workers Benefit Protection Act (which is an amendment to the Age Discrimination in Employment Act), everyone 40 and over has 21 days to consider a severance package before being expected to sign it. And then, no matter when in that 21-day span they put pen to paper, they have 7 days in which to reconsider and change their minds. Are you younger than 40? That's okay because, to be on the safe side, employers trend in the direction of having a policy that allows all employees to have that same time frame. They just might not tell you about it. Or that detail might be part of the small print portion of the program. Either way, if you think you might get nothing if you don't sign then and there, don't give in to that pressure—even if it's only coming from within yourself.

At the moment of truth, this last piece of advice might be the hardest to follow. Think about it: You're in shock, you've just been told that your services are no longer needed by the people and organization you've cared about. Your feelings are hurt, to say the least. And these two caring, sincere people compassionately slide the severance package across the desk toward you. And there might even be a check clipped to the envelope—for more money than you've ever seen in one single paycheck. And, let's face it, this may be the last check you'll be seeing for a while. And one with your name on the Pay to the Order Of line. (You know that—job or no job—you'll still be writing plenty of your own in upcoming months. That money will come in very handy very soon.)

It could take a super-human effort to push the check back to them and take the proposed contract (or ask for a copy of it) so that you can think about it in calmer moments. After all, these severance packages are all the same, right? Maybe yes, maybe no. And, Sklover says, the severance packages might be all the same, but there's only one of you. And you have your own unique set of circumstances. And those circumstances deserve to be considered before signing away your rights to return to the company with legitimate claims:

- You're within days of completing an important project. And you'd like to have time to finish it so that you can at least have a success story to tell in future interviews.

- The termination meeting is happening toward the end of the month. If you delay that actual termination date by just a few days into the following month, you and your family are eligible for an additional month's health insurance.
- The termination meeting is happening toward the end of the year. If you delay the actual date by just a few days into the following year, your tenure span at this company will look better on your resumé.
- If you delay your termination by just a few days into the following year, you might also be eligible for a better pension, bonus, and stock option arrangement.
- If you are able to put off the termination for a while so that you look like you still have a job while you're looking for a job, that could make you more attractive to other hiring managers.
- You have a workers' comp claim in process, and that is much more valuable to you than the severance package.
- You have reason to think that you have been discriminated against for other reasons. Or you don't think you do, but a review with an attorney could reveal a detail that would change the game significantly.
- You don't know what you want. Maybe you would rather have paid tuition or relocation expenses instead of a severance payout that amounts to only a fraction of that value.
- You need time to think it through—with the help of a calm mind (preferably your own), your spouse or life partner, or an attorney who knows about these things.
- You can afford to wait. They may not have told you this part, but you do have time.

The best thing you can do:
Listen carefully and take excellent notes of the meeting.

The worst thing you can do:
Get emotional, thereby harming your ability to negotiate.

The first thing you should do:
Maintain perspective. Sklover says, "This is not hearing that you have terminal cancer or that a loved one has been in a car accident. This is something that you will survive no matter what."

CHAPTER 10

Ask for Special Treatment

The following true story probably happens much more frequently than we know. It's just not the kind of thing that tends to get around. A senior vice president of HR was overseeing a massive layoff in a very large company. As she was reviewing the names of the employees who were selected to be terminated, she noticed one particular man who had a special situation. He had been diagnosed with terminal cancer. He was still at work, but everyone knew that it wouldn't be long before he could no longer perform the tasks of his job. This wasn't the reason why he was on the list; the fact that he was scheduled to be laid off was coincidental. But when the HR exec spotted his name, she put her foot down, saying, "There's no way we're going to lay him off!" And they decided to put him on permanent disability instead, sparing him and his family one more blow of bad news.

When large companies populate huge lists of employees they have determined to lay off, they don't always stop to think of what each specific employee's circumstances are or what additional value the employee represents to the organization and any projects that might be underway. As a result, some very special cases get folded in among the rest. And you may be one of them.

Naturally, these companies want to push the process along. And they've spent a lot of money on consultants and lawyers hammering out the wording of the severance packages just so. As a result, they're probably not going to be amenable to any custom tinkering from an employee who might be jockeying for special treatment. But if you have a special case, you might as well at least ask for a special arrangement.

It certainly couldn't hurt. And they could actually agree to customize. According to Sklover, these special situations could be cause for some alterations of your agreement—in your favor:

- **Pipeline value:** You may have some importance to the company in the future. Perhaps you're in the middle of a high-value business deal, or your presence at a meeting is extremely important. Perhaps they need your help in smoothing the transition of critical client relations to the new team taking over from you. Or all your essential working knowledge is still in your head, and you need to pass it on to your replacement. All these things take both time and your commitment to do an excellent job. That has value to both you and the company.

- **Contractual expressions:** Throughout your tenure at the company, you may have been promised certain things that you have yet to receive. These can include unpaid bonuses, reimbursement for monies you have laid out, vesting of stock or stock options, promotions, commissions, annual performance reviews, educational assistance, and time off. If you sign your severance agreement, you would be releasing your right to claim these things. So bring them up now, before you sign away your rights to those items.

- **Defamatory effects:** Getting laid off happens to the best of us. And it's not as shameful as it used to be. But still, depending on the circumstances, and where you are in your career, that little item on your resumé could give recruiters and hiring managers cause to pause—and then maybe pass you by. You could be facing additional difficulty if your termination was abrupt, if you were heading up a department that was closed down completely, or if you think that your boss might not be an enthusiastically positive reference.

- **Discrimination or interference with vested benefits:** The chances are excellent that you haven't been discriminated against because of your age, race, gender, or sexual preference. But if you reasonably believe that you have been, or if you think that being laid off is interfering with your rights to benefits that are due you, bring that up now.

- **Retaliatory responses:** If you had refused to take part in illegal activities or had "blown the whistle" on the company's activities, and then you got laid off, you might have a case. This isn't the time to try to use the suspicion of retaliation as a do-it-yourself negotiation for a better severance agreement. Be sure to consult an attorney in these circumstances.

- **Unusual, extreme need:** Remember the employee with terminal cancer? That's an unusual or extreme need. But it doesn't have to be that extreme for you to perhaps have a circumstance that would be cause to review your severance package. Think about how your dismissal might present difficulties for you that others would not be facing. Your unusual circumstances might be cause for revisiting the language of your package and improving its considerations in your favor.

Get expert help as you consider how the legal particulars of the severance agreement will affect your life and career. Keep in mind that your company sought the expert advice of attorneys who have done this many times. You're probably not an attorney, and you probably haven't done this before. Don't go this alone.

CHAPTER 11

A Word About Noncompete Agreements

Noncompete agreements can quite literally have you coming and going. If you're not careful, you could be signing away your ability to earn a living doing what you do best. But if you're really smart, you can turn that agreement into added cash in your severance package. If you're not so smart, you could turn that agreement into leaden handcuffs that prohibit you from practicing your career anywhere else for a certain amount of time.

The most common times when you could be asked to sign a noncompete agreement are when you're about to start a new job (where they have you coming), and when you've been asked to leave your job in a layoff situation (where they have you going). When you start the new job, the noncompete agreement doesn't seem like such an unreasonable request. This is a permanent (insert "air quotes" here) job you just took on, and all the signs are that the company is flourishing in a flourishing economy. They've bent over backward to bring you onboard—maybe even offering a signing bonus. What could possibly go wrong? Sure, you'll sign the noncompete. You won't be going anywhere, and you certainly wouldn't want to do anything to harm the competitiveness of your new employer. Plus you want to look like a cooperative team player. Where's the pen?

That old noncompete could come back to haunt you the day they call you into the room with the closed door to break the bad news to you. That noncompete is still in place. But you have to make yourself as marketable as you can in a new job-search world of competing candidates who aren't encumbered by non-competes. Or you're asked to sign a new or different noncompete as a condition of your severance agreement.

This might be the time for a lawyer (your lawyer, not theirs) to help you understand how binding noncompetes are under your state law. But in the meantime, see whether you can talk your former employer into reconsidering some of the parameters of the noncompete they're shoving across the table at you.

If your skillsets are transferable to any kind of company in any kind of industry, perhaps they can delete any comprehensive language that might prohibit you from doing the same job at all and insert some specific language that discusses particular competing companies. Always make sure there's a time limit here, by the way.

If your skillsets are industry-specific, which could truly pose a direct competitive threat to your former employer, perhaps they can modify the language to allow you to work for smaller companies or companies that cater to a different kind of market that your former company has no interest in.

If your noncompete agreement prohibits you from working in similar companies or industries doing similar things, perhaps you can arrange language that limits that prohibition to a certain number of months.

Whatever agreement you strike with your former employer, remember that your promise not to compete with them is most likely worth real money to them. Otherwise they wouldn't be bothered to use valuable lawyer time to craft the language tying you down. Your ability to work freely in the job market is worth real money to you, as well. If they want to tie your hands, even if it's only by just a few months, that should cost them extra.

At least it's worth a try.

The best thing you can do:
Assume everything is negotiable.

The worst thing you can do:
Sign anything without thoroughly considering your options.

The first thing you should do:
Understand what you're signing.

CHAPTER 12

Not That It Matters to You, but It Hurts for Them, Too

When it comes to getting laid off, there are three main possible sources of shock:

1. The fact that you are being laid off at all
2. The provisions in your severance package
3. The way the layoff was handled

This discussion focuses on why the layoff was handled the way it was handled. The unfortunate fact of life is that by the time the next few years are behind us, companies will be much better at laying off people more humanely. Nothing like practice and experience to make perfect. Unfortunately, right now, even though modern layoffs have been going on for 30 years, many employers are still newbies at this. And they're scared to death of bungling it so badly that they will be sued. And what you might be experiencing on the recipient's end is the latest chapter in the epic struggle between humanely considering the feelings of the employee and the demands of protecting a company's legal derriere. Guess which side is winning.

There is, however, a growing collection of best practices around layoffs, and some of the most people-centric companies have found a way to be as thoughtful toward the employees' feelings as possible. But there are still way too many examples of security guards or managers marching the freshly axed employees to their cars, laying on blankets of rage, humiliation, and hurt feelings over that foundation of shock, confusion, and lack of closure the employee is already feeling. Who needs that?

Libby Sartain, a Bastrop, Texas-based HR advisor, who used to lead the HR functions of Southwest Airlines and Yahoo!, says that when that happens, that's often a sign of the legal department calling the shots—with HR having to comply.

"What usually happens is that there are one or two people you think might cause a problem during the layoff process, and so you manage to those two contingencies rather than the 98% of the people who wouldn't be problems," she says. "When you're laying off 10%, 20%, or 30% of your workforce, the legal department is going to get involved. And legal is managing to protect the company, which often means that HR gets the pressure to treat everyone exactly the same."

So the 98% get frog-marched out to their car on the off chance that a member of the 2% contingent will freak out and do something regrettable.

Even if management doesn't call in the militia, does it really have to be so abrupt? Sartain says, sometimes, yes.

"The number one concern is that people will walk out with the company's intellectual property," she says. In the time it takes you to say good-bye to the kitchen staff, you could be downloading onto a thumb drive the schematics of next year's top-secret flagship release. And that is a real, legitimate concern.

Most often, though, says Sartain, management recognizes that once you've gotten the news that you're history, you have already moved on elsewhere in your heart and head. And so even if you've been given two weeks' notice—at least long enough to catch up on all those emails and let your core business partners know that you will be passing the ball to someone else—you would be spending much of that time thinking about your next new job and looking for it. So why not start now?

Employees who work for companies (generally with 100 full-time employees or more) that are starting a massive layoff initiative are covered by the WARN Act (the Worker Adjustment and Retraining Notification Act), which requires employers to give 60 days' notice that a layoff is on the horizon. Some companies use the WARN Act to immediately slough off individual unwanted employees by telling them that this is their 60-day notice, but here's payment for those 60 days right now. So, see ya.

It's an unfortunate and unpleasant situation when you are in a room where everyone's heart is breaking but no one is able to say how they really feel. The people who are laying you off aren't allowed to. And you may not be given the chance to. It's all very legal, you understand.

So, again, as the years unfold, we'll probably get better at this. As employees we'll finally get the idea that no job is secure, no matter what. And as managers, we'll finally be able to treat these people we care about with the kindness, courtesy, and dignity they deserve.

But in the meantime, if you find yourself being give the bum's rush with truly unnecessary haste, just forgive them if (or when) you can. They may not know what they're doing. Yet.

The best thing you can do:
Understand that the layoff process is probably driven by a script mandated by the legal department.

The worst thing you can do:
Take its treatment of you as a reflection of what the company really thinks of you.

The first thing you should do:
Resolve to put the circumstances of the actual layoff behind you, because that memory will be the one that could hurt the most as you try to move forward in your life.

PART IV

WHEN YOU'VE BEEN LAID OFF

CHAPTER 13

Financial: Control Your Spending

You might not be able to control what's coming in (for right now), but you have absolute control over what's going out. And reconsidering how you buy things will put you back in the driver's seat of your life, without significantly changing your lifestyle—unless, of course, you have to sell the yacht at a loss.

Finding ways to save money is actually a source of immediate gratification, says Greg Karp, author of *Living Rich by Spending Smart: How to Get More of What You Really Want.* He breaks it down like this:

- **Magnitude:** You get to keep more out of every dollar you save than every dollar you earn. (Don't forget the taxes and Social Security.)

- **Speed:** Cutting spending is much faster than earning new money. You can start seeing results immediately, which has got to be good for your frame of mind. Cut your gym membership, for example (but still exercise, because your mood is still important). The instant you make that decision, you've put that money in your pocket. How long would it take you to make that same amount (counting, of course, taxes and Social Security)?

- **Control:** You make dozens of buying decisions every day. Right now you're probably not making too many earning decisions. Maybe one, which is to keep your job. And even that decision isn't something you have total control over. "The ultimate control," says Karp, "is on the spending side of the equation."

- **Emotional gratification:** Isn't it nice to know that you still have executive decision-making powers over some essential aspects of your life? You are in control over your spending. And you can give yourself the satisfaction of exercising that control without completely denying yourself those things that you love (except, of course, the aforementioned yacht)—especially in the three areas that are essential to living in a modern, high-tech world during a crisis.

Here's how.

Food

- Don't eat out at all. (Don't worry; it's not forever. It's just for now. Restaurants won't completely disappear. Let other people support that service sector while you're riding out this downtime.)

- Don't feel that you have to choke down what you hate just because it's on sale. That's no way to live.

- Don't go to the supermarket when you need things; go to your pantry, basement, attic, closet, bedroom. When things you need, use, and love go on sale, stock up. You don't have to load up on provisions enough to cover you for a circumnavigation. Just enough to cover you for 12 weeks, which is what Karp says is the typical cycle when things go back on sale. Surely, you can find space somewhere in your home for four months' worth of toilet paper and paper towels.

- When the weekly supermarket circular comes around, pay extra close attention to the front and back pages. Karp said that those are where markets list their "loss leaders," items that they may actually be selling below cost.

- Use coupons only as part of your stockpiling strategy, not as a shopping strategy. Saving 5 to 50 cents on a single item that you wouldn't necessarily buy when you had money really doesn't make sense now. But if you use the coupons to enhance the savings of something you're buying in stockpiling mode, you can save as much as 75% to even 100% off the cost of the item.

- Use your loyalty cards. Let the privacy fiends shriek at the thought of someone building a dossier on your toilet paper habits. Who cares?

Insurance

- Shop around; you can save money immediately. According to Karp, you have no reason to be brand loyal when it comes to insurance. The Consumer Federation of America has found no correlation between what you pay in a premium and the quality of service you can expect to receive in return.
- If you have had term life insurance for a long time, investigate whether you can get a better deal now. Life insurance rates have followed the same path as consumer electronics prices. They've plummeted in recent years.
- If you have whole life insurance, get term life insurance.
- Make sure you get the change securely in place before you cancel the existing policy.
- Raise your deductibles on your home and auto insurance. Karp recommends at least $1,000 for the car and $2,500 for the home. (You don't even want to be tempted to file a claim for anything smaller anyway. Karp says to remember that insurance is to protect you from financial disaster, not from life's little bummers.)
- As for health insurance, once you start seeing the COBRA payments, you're going to want to change that in a big hurry. Determine if you might qualify for memberships to organizations that offer their own group health insurance plans. If

you're married to someone who is covered at work, great! Your next step is an obvious one. If you are engaged to someone who is covered, you might want to consider a quick elopement. (No insurance fraud here, people, you have to be in love already.) It will disappoint the folks, but when you think about the cost of a full-on wedding, perhaps a post-nuptial weenie roast would be a better reception anyway. Even better if the weenies were a supermarket's loss leader for that week.

Telecommunications

This could be painful. I say "reduce," but Karp says "cancel." "Before I put the pink slip on the table when I got home, I'd have a phone in hand canceling services," he says. Ouch, but he has a point. "Your first job now is reclaiming power and getting on firm financial ground so you can live to fight another day." Can't argue with that. But let's look at options anyway:

- **Cable television:** Karp says "cancel." I say, "See what you're really watching and cancel the rest." Do you really need all those premium movie channels? Or do you just need to watch your stock go to hell on the CNBC crawl? If you can, try to cancel all those channels that focus on murder, mayhem, arrests, and people trying to recover from drug addiction. All that negativity is just plain bad for your brain. Hmm. That doesn't leave many channels, does it? Maybe you might want to cancel cable television after all.

- **Subscription movie services:** Karp says "cancel." I say "keep." My current subscription price is $16.99 a month for unlimited movies, three at a time. That's less than two theater movies if I go alone. Not to mention gas; and certainly not to mention overpriced concession stand junk food. For less than $20 a month, you can have unlimited movies delivered straight to your door, with enough variety to keep everyone in your family happy. You can make your own popcorn by pouring plain kernels in a lunch bag and throwing it in the microwave.

- **Cell phone:** You can cancel and keep it at the same time. Assuming that you won't be slapped with hideous termination fees (yeah, right), you can keep your cell phone number and transfer it to a prepaid phone that you load minutes onto as you need them. Once the must-have accessory for itinerants, drug dealers, and people with rock-bottom credit ratings, prepaid phones have entered the community of respectable people. They may be more expensive per minute than your more conventional account (or maybe not), but you won't be using your cell phone that much anyway, and you can control the minutes you choose to use.

- **Your landline:** Even Karp doesn't want to take away your Internet (connectivity is crucial to employability), so consider using Internet-based phone services to save a lot on your landline expenses. If you have a very fast and dependable online connection, companies like Vonage offer services at prices ($15 a month) that put conventional phone companies to shame. And new companies, such as Magic Jack, have prices ($20 a year) that could put Vonage to shame. (See, now you can afford your movie by mail subscription.)

Speaking of subscriptions, Karp also recommends that you scrutinize your monthly statements for automatically recurring charges. For instance, that item that you ordered after watching an infomercial has conveniently placed you on a recurring charge plan that you neglected to notice when you clicked Confirm on the order page. (Personally, I have a stack of cellophane-wrapped DVDs of exercises for rock-hard abs, when I thought I had ordered only one. But a new box comes every month. Guess it's time to cancel.)

And, when it comes to magazine subscriptions, don't let yourself get rattled by those renewal envelopes that scream "Third and Final Notice!" First of all, if you look at your mailing label, you might notice you still have six months left before your subscription runs out anyway. Second, what are they going to do if you let your subscription run out? Refuse to renew you? I don't think so. Third, let your subscription run out. You can still read the magazine at the library. (The postal carrier isn't going to think you're a deadbeat with those alarming envelopes. All your neighbors are getting them, too.)

All this control isn't about self-denial. It's about reminding yourself how small, simple decisions you make every day can make a huge difference in your financial peace of mind. As Karp says, "If we use this time in our lives to reconsider all the decisions we make about our money, we'll emerge feeling good about ourselves and with greater self-respect. Plugging the leaks of wasteful spending and redirecting that money to things we really care about is not about deprivation. It's about liberation."

The best thing you can do:
Remember that you are still in control of your finances.

The worst thing you can do:
Worry about other people's opinion of you as you start cutting expenses.

The first thing you should do:
Sit down, take out a pen, make a list of expenses, and then start crossing things off that you know you can immediately save money on.

CHAPTER 14

What Do I Do with All This Rage?

Be glad, first of all, that you're feeling all those feelings. As your mother might have told you, "If it's itching, that means it's healing." That principle works for the skinned knee. It works for the scraped spirit, as well. You're not crazy for being crazed with rage. And you're not crazy for being relieved and even happy at the same time. It's all part of the big mess that's been thrown at you when you were laid off. Now that big mess has taken up residence in your head.

Let's take a moment to parse some of the emotions that might be roiling through your system right now:

- **You feel suddenly extraneous.** How can that be? Until just yesterday, your managers had been successfully convincing you that your efforts and focus were essential to the company's mission-critical objectives. So you've allowed yourself to be overworked for years. And suddenly the company can do without you? That just doesn't make sense.

- **You can't make sense of things.** Your brain isn't working for you the way it did just yesterday. If you're a knowledge professional, you're used to using your brain to find patterns and solutions. And there's no pattern that emerges to help you figure out what just happened.

- **You're mad.**
  - You're mad at your management for lying to you. Oh. They didn't outright lie to you? They just didn't tell you that someone pondered your specific value to the organization and then letter by letter put your name on the bye-bye list?

And then no one told you, even though they knew? Even though they smiled at you passing by the coffee pot just yesterday afternoon? You're mad.

- You're mad at yourself for not having seen it coming. What good is that much-celebrated brain of yours anyway if it can't protect you from joblessness?
- You're mad at your former coworkers who haven't called. You feel like they've changed the channel on you but you're still broadcasting.
- You're mad at your nonwork friends who won't stop calling you, trying to jolly you out of your state of mind, telling you they understand (as if), and to look on the bright side of things.
- You're mad that the senior executives whose ego, libido, recklessness, and/or fecklessness have run your beloved company right into the ground. They still have their mansions and golden parachutes. You have severance. Such as it is.
- You're mad that you listened to the wrong people.
- You're mad that you didn't listen to yourself.
- You're mad that your spouse, who still has a job, doesn't entirely get why you're so mad all the time.

- **And you're happy.**
  - You're happy that your spouse still has a job and is spared this experience of dealing with all the uncertainty and conflicting emotions.
  - You're happy that now you don't have to worry anymore about getting laid off.
  - You're happy that you don't have to face your former coworkers until you're ready—that you can process through these feelings in private.

- You're happy that you don't have to go back to work the next morning like all those thousands of people who are lining up on the highways, bus stops, and train platforms.
- You're happy that now you can take some time and listen to your own thoughts for once.
- You're happy that that company's problems aren't yours anymore.
- You're happy to have this chance at a fresh start.

Those are a lot of competing emotions to hold in one, shocked heart. And you might be thinking that maybe you're a little nuts to be carrying so many feelings that logically should be canceling each other out. And even if you know you're not losing your mind for having these conflicting feelings, it's beginning to feel as if you don't do something about them—and soon—you could lose whatever semblance of sanity that you might have left.

"Of course you are going to feel all these conflicting emotions," says Meredith Kaplan, a Palm Beach Gardens, Florida, certified professional coach and licensed mental health counselor. "It's essential that you recognize all these feelings and not deny them. If you repress any of this, you could end up sinking into a serious depression."

Kaplan says that it's important to recognize all the many things your job represented to you. While you've been focusing so much on the role you've played in your company, it's easy to have perhaps overlooked all the roles your job played in your life.

"Our work touches on all the levels of Maslow's hierarchy of needs," says Kaplan. "When you lose your job, you start to worry about the most basic needs of food, clothing, and shelter. Then you can track the impact of your job loss through all the levels, right up to the meta-needs of love, belonging, purpose, and self-actualization."

It only follows that the impact of losing your job is larger than just merely losing your job. It's hitting all aspects of your life. You need a mission, a plan, and a team to help you carry out this next phase of your life—even if your immediate goal is to process the pain with your self-esteem, sense of purpose, sanity, and family intact. This is your key project for your immediate present. Now is the time to let your executive skills serve you well, as you follow Kaplan's advice:

- **Assess the state of your life.** Kaplan says that when people have the time to stop and consider who they are outside the binding, busy context of their jobs, they discover that they might have let all the other essentials of healthful living fall out of balance: their family relationships, their commitment to community, their eating and exercise habits, their spending. When you slow down long enough to look closely at who you've become, you may be afraid of what you might see. Try not to judge yourself too harshly (if you're tempted to go in that direction). Just use the new information as important data to help you reorganize your priorities and discover how to live the rest of your life according to your values.

- **Reacquaint yourself with your own values.** Recognize that in the years that you've been so busy, you may have changed so much that your sense of who you are and what's important to you have been long outdated.

- **Reacquaint yourself with what has been your life's purpose.** That probably hasn't changed, at least not much. And that's okay, because your sense of purpose should transcend the short-term phases of your life. Unless your core sense of purpose dates back to—or, worse, was inspired by—Don Johnson in *Miami Vice*. Then you might want to start from scratch.

- **Remind yourself of the contributions you've made, the skills you've built, and what makes you unique in the world.** If this idea makes you cringe like a Stuart Smalley moment on *Saturday Night Live,* okay. Go with it, anyway. There have been forces at work to hammer away at your self-esteem and make you forget that you actually do have a place in the world. So you need to counteract them. "Self-praising is an important part of regrouping," says Kaplan. As you relaunch your job interview process, you're going to want to sound like you're talking about yourself when you discuss your strengths, achievements, and abilities, not someone else. So keep those ideas about yourself positive, current, and in the forefront of your mind.

- **Stay away from pain-numbing, negatively mood-altering behaviors.** You know what those are: drugs, alcohol, over-eating, undereating, not sleeping, sleeping too much. Kaplan says that even if you have to feel the pain of the layoff full on, keeping your state of awareness unaltered will process the pain faster and help you stay aware and alert to opportunities as they begin to come your way. Vigorous exercise is a great way to purge rage, but you already knew that. So, what's holding you up?

- **Enlist the help and support of cooperative and nonjudgmental friends and family.** People are going to want to help, and they need you to tell them how. You don't need anyone to tell you that they understand what you're going through. You might just need to be reassured that your friends aren't criticizing you for your feelings of uncertainty and anger. Says Kaplan: "Any kind of loss is ameliorated through intimate relationships with close friends and family members with whom you can be yourself. It's such a comfort knowing that there's someone who will sincerely say, 'I'm right beside you. You're not doing this alone.'"

- **Keep doing the things you loved doing before.** You may not get as much pleasure out of them right away. How easy is it to get all excited about Guitar Hero, or even the community garden, when you're not sure where your next paycheck is coming from? But those feelings will come back. "Build in time to do those things that give you positive emotions. That will help you find a place within you where you start feeling stronger, which, in turn, will help you move forward more quickly," says Kaplan. Two things to remember about this piece of advice: So many of the things in life that give us pleasure are either free or they've already been paid for (or at least you're still paying for them on your credit card). So you might as well enjoy them! The second thing is this: If you just can't find it within you to love what you loved before, get to a therapist quickly. Depression might be taking hold.

- **Build up your resiliency and restore your faith in yourself with the attitude of "what can I do to make a difference today."** You have a choice, says Kaplan, to be either victimized by what happened to you and stay that way. Or rally the forces of the skills and knowledge that had brought you to that marvelous job (you know, the one you just lost) and use them to the greater good. Negative emotions of helplessness drain your energy and choke off your access to solution-oriented thinking. Staying in touch with your very real ability to affect change in other peoples' lives—not to mention your own—creates a positive influence on your brain that is self-perpetuating.

- **Work with others to get the job done—and get a job.** Kaplan recommends working with coaches and leader-managed support groups to help you focus on the task at hand, which is to get a new job. Other people who are focused on the exact same goals you are will give you the support, ideas, connections, and accountability expectations to keep you on track. It's much better to hear your group members ask "Did you make your five phone calls today?" than to hear that from your spouse. Kaplan also says that support groups benefit from having a leader so that they stay focused and task-oriented and resist the pull of sliding into ruminating over the outrage of getting laid off, who said what, who said what back, who should have said what when, and so forth.

Your emotional reactions are your leftover legacy from the job you just lost. How you choose to deal with them could be the most important executive decision you will ever make. At least until you get your new job.

The best thing you can do:
Take action. It's extremely empowering to know that you are still in control.

The worst thing you can do:
Stay angry or repress that emotion. Those two approaches will just immobilize you.

The first thing you should do:
Acknowledge all your feelings and emotions associated with your loss.

Voice of Experience: Anna

I had worked for a privately held company as a straight commission salesperson since 1991, helping it grow to a $55 million business. When the owners decided to sell it to a publicly held company a couple of years ago, I was actually a cheerleader for that change. And I was very happy for the original owners, who walked away with millions. They deserved it.

At first things looked pretty good with the new company, but it wasn't long before I could see signs that the new management was running the company into the ground; they were just incompetent. My boss and I watched as they burned through money, and we couldn't understand how the business could sustain it. Signs of trouble were everywhere. People had begun to be laid off at corporate, and the leadership was just being really irresponsible and stupid. It was like they were playing with Monopoly money. They didn't seem to care about the company and its employees, as long as they were taking home millions themselves.

I decided to relocate from Colorado to California because I believed that I could grow my business even faster there. So I called my general manager and said, "Can I confidently make this move?" My husband had just been laid off, and we didn't want to buy a house without certainty that this would be a good business move for me.

My GM reassured me that everything was great and that I could confidently make the commitment. We had just closed escrow when they announced that they were closing down the business.

Fortunately, I had decided on my own to talk with two of my competitors about possibilities. So by the time the company made the announcement, I had two deals to choose from. My industry isn't all that big. And because I've been doing this for 28 years, I had a strong reputation in my field and good relationships even with my competitors. Because I didn't have a noncompete agreement with my original company, I was free to talk with anyone I wanted.

I didn't feel bad at all about interviewing with my competitors because that's part of taking responsibility for myself. What I was doing for myself was exactly what the management of my company should have been doing for itself: taking responsibility for what's happening and doing something about it.

I'm still really angry at the way the new owners of my old company ran a healthy, viable business into the ground. But my new employer tells me that within a year I'll come to realize that this new company is a better fit for me anyway. I have gone from the dumbest company in the business to the smartest company in the business. I can see that.

In the meantime, I read the old company's chat rooms on Yahoo! now and then. And I see how the working conditions at corporate are deteriorating. They have become very difficult to work for and are managing their employees in a very aggressive and abusive way. The people who have gone are telling the people who are still there, "Leave! You need to leave! There are industries and people who will appreciate you and not browbeat you." But now people are getting scared because they might have waited so long that there might not be very much out there.

The best thing you can do:
Figure out how you're relevant to the company's bottom line. And if you discover that you're not relevant, find a way to get relevant—figure out how your skills support the company's profitability. Or find a new company where your skills do relate directly to the profitability.

The worst thing you can do:
Do nothing.

The first thing you should do:
Do something and do it right now. Take control over what is going to happen to you. Don't wait until your hand is forced. You absolutely lose your power then.

CHAPTER 15

The Kids Can Handle the Truth

As hard as it is to hear the news that you have lost your job, it could be even harder to pass the news on to your family (especially the kids, no matter how old they are). Just when you've been saddled with the shock of losing your job—calling into action your maximum resilience, clarity of mind, courage and hope—here's another wake-up call for you: How you treat your children during this time of family crisis could affect their own development and the prospects of your family for decades to come.

If you come from a family tradition that says that children are resilient and they can get over anything, that kids are so self-absorbed that they don't notice what's going on around them, or that kids will believe any fable you dish out to them, or that kids can be protected from adult reality by simple silence, it's time to change your mind about children even as you're being forced to change your mind about yourself and your immediate world.

Kids may be young. They may be distracted by insignificant things such as games, toys, what's on TV, fashion. But they're not stupid. They care—even though they might not look like they do. And they're watching you. Right now.

How you handle life during a crisis is just as significant a lesson—if not more so—than how you relish life during great times. (In fact, how you relish life during a crisis is also an important lesson, come to think of it, as you show your children that happiness is within reach no matter what the situation is.) Seize this period in your family's life as an opportunity to teach them valuable lessons of hope that will be passed down through generations in times to come—good times to come, and bad times.

There are just a few things to keep in mind.

The kids know more than you've told them. You might think you're protecting them from difficult truths. But in fact, they may be protecting you from the fact that they know more than you think, and that they're carrying a heavy load of worry all by themselves. Looking back on the months preceding our own father's layoff, I remember my brother and me watchfully measuring the level of anger coming in through the front door at the end of every working day and casting worried glances at each other. "Is Dad mad?" was a frequent question we asked each other day after day. There was an unexpressed tension in the house we hadn't experienced since our mother had died ten years earlier. And, of course, the unspoken questions between us were "Is Dad mad at us?" and "What can we do to make Dad less mad?" In the meantime, Dad had no idea how tension would ripple through the house like heat waves as he entered the foyer. He was a good dad; he was handling things. We were good children. We were protecting him from our own anxieties. How good we were all being. How utterly alone we were and unable to help each other out.

Kids have more ways of taking information in beyond just what you have explicitly told them. Depending on their ages and levels of maturity, they can be absorbing emotional data in the house like little Dopplers. They're not being nosy or selfish; they're being normal. Their very survival depends on Mom and Dad keeping it together. As the children grow older, they're augmenting their intuitive skills with overhearing anguished late-night conversations, understanding snippets of news on CNN, listening for strains of "We're In the Money" or "Stormy Weather" after NPR's market report, or hearing that their friends' parents have lost their jobs.

The less you tell them, the more they will come up with their own explanations. If your kids are prone to catastrophize the slightest kitchen mishap as a metaphor of how the whole universe is spinning madly into disaster, just imagine how they're internalizing and interpreting the growing tension at home.

Or if they merrily tend to assume everything is wonderful, orderly, and abundant until otherwise notified, you can't really blame them when they get upset when they hear that they can't go on the annual ski trip with their friends. They're not being selfish or immature; they just don't know the facts as they pertain specifically to your family. But they still know more than you think they do. Even if it's just their intuition whispering in their ear.

If you lie to your children, telling them everything is fine, you're teaching them to grow up not trusting their intuition, says Ellen Raynes Berman, Psy.D., a Stamford, Connecticut-based therapist who works with children and adolescents. And that's a disservice as much as it could be overloading them with the gory details of grownup finances. Intuition is a tool they're going to need their whole lives. After all, it may be their intuition that will help them prepare for their own careers-in-flux a couple of decades from now.

If you tell them more than they need to know, in terms that are beyond their ability to understand, you might be giving them the early experience that they are helpless in the face of life's challenges. They could be taking on board the conclusions that they have no power to make a difference, that hard work and dedication is rewarded with rejection and disappointment, that people have value only as long as you need them, or there's simply no point in trying anymore at all. And to think all this time you thought they were worried about fashion and computer games.

Decide now what the themes of this family saga will be. As I write this chapter, the survivors of the 2008 Mumbai attacks are beginning to tell their stories. And I keep hearing, "Thank God! Thank God!" They can barely contain the swells of gratitude as they also praise the strength, professionalism, and courage of the commandos who put their own lives at risk to rescue them. They are looking directly into the camera and telling the rest of us around the world, "Don't be afraid."

Modern life is full of horror stories, to be sure. If your children are old enough to remember 9/11, they already know that. They may have also discovered themselves that there are always at least two equally legitimate ways to tell a story. One way is to focus on the random horror of the acts of selfish or evil people, and how innocents get tragically caught up in it. The other way is of hope, resilience, endurance, courage, gratitude, teamwork, focus, and the big-picture perspective of "We'll be alright. We might not know how right now, but we will be okay. Don't be afraid."

Decide which perspective and epic family narrative will best equip everyone (you, your spouse, and your children) for a successful future. And then gather the stories, vocabulary, and direct experiences to reinforce the message that good times come and go, but then, good times come back again. And in the meantime, there is always plenty to be grateful for.

Remember that your own behaviors model your beliefs and life philosophies. The kids are watching and taking their cues from you. As much as they want the truth from you, they also want guidance as to how to handle the truth. If your family culture celebrates faith in a higher power, generosity, community participation, and optimism, don't see this layoff as a test of your beliefs. See it as an opportunity to demonstrate the power of your beliefs through your actions.

Be emotionally authentic, but just remember that if you freak out, so will your kids. If you continue spending money like it was 2005, so will your kids. If you show through your actions that getting laid off can't touch your core sense of self-esteem or cause you to pull back on your generosity of love, community spirit, and faith, your children will use the memory of this as a pillar of strength that will last their entire lives.

Make sure the lessons and expectations are consistent with your family culture, regardless of whether the times are good or bad. Berman says that she doesn't believe that children should have an extraordinary role in making things better or easier for the family during more difficult times that might come from a layoff. "Keep adult problems the purview of adults," she says. "Kids just can't solve adult problems, and so don't treat them like miniature adults."

Berman says that now is an excellent time to be teaching them what you probably would be teaching them anyway: the importance of not wasting things; turning off electricity and faucets; respect for other people and their time, belongings, and feelings; their roles within their communities (whether that community is their immediate family circle, their friends, or the town they live in).

Berman also says that it probably isn't a good idea to expect children to contribute to the family finances. And, she says, you should still give them their allowance, if that were a pre-layoff practice. "The most important thing is predictability and stability," she says. "That is how they learn to feel safe and to trust."

This is also the time, she says, to remind them that hard work is its own reward. Excellent performance and superior ratings (or in their case, good grades) might not guarantee the advancement or external rewards that you—or they—might logically expect. But they feed and demonstrate your self-respect and sense of control in your life. And those are things that no one can take away.

The best thing you can do:
Give your children the age-appropriate information they need to feel safe.

The worst thing you can do:
Be a bad role model for handling anxiety and depression.

The first thing you should do:
Assess your financial situation so that you don't do or say things that are panic-driven.

CHAPTER 16

Good Things to Remember

You have heard of "teachable moments" at work—those highly charged (usually unfortunate) incidents that give leaders and their teams the chance to stop and talk about what the lasting lessons might be. When you've been laid off, you have one big teachable moment to bring home to the family. Although this most certainly isn't the teachable moment you would choose, it's yours anyway. So make the most of it to give your children positive, confidence-building lessons that will carry them throughout their lives—in both bad and good times that are sure to come:

- Self-worth doesn't depend on status, status symbols, or job titles.
- Money is not the way to measure value.
- Fun can be free.
- Money-tight times won't last forever.
- Money worries might change your life, but they won't wreck it.
- Positive thinking leads to creative, solution-oriented thinking.
- Everyone inside the family circle is safe—including the pets.
- Everyone inside the family circle is important—including the pets.
- Teamwork starts at home.
- Uncertainty doesn't mean certain catastrophe.
- It's fun to find creative ways to save money.

- Manage stress with games, exercise, laughter, and quiet times—no alcohol, drugs, yelling, arguing, or hurting others.
- Don't let others manipulate you into feeling anxious.
- You don't need a job to make a difference.
- Happiness doesn't depend on having money.
- You can always make things better for someone else.
- Little kindnesses can make a big difference.
- Borrowing (anything but money) can be better than buying.
- Sharing is fun.
- Don't judge others; everyone is coping the best way they know how.
- Discipline helps to make dreams come true.
- Later can be better than now.
- Later doesn't mean never.
- What you have is not the same as who you are.
- There is always plenty to be grateful for.

Voice of Experience: Charles

I worked for a family-owned real estate and agricultural business for 10 years, starting as an accountant, progressing to a comptroller position. I have two master's degrees, one in information systems, which the company paid for. I had a long-term career plan that one day I would take over the IT department. Everyone in the company bought into that plan, so I thought I was safe.

Over the past few years, it had invested heavily into real estate development and put a lot of its eggs in that one basket. As the housing market collapsed, the company started going through some tremendously difficult times. I knew things were bad and was aware that companywide layoffs were on the horizon. But I honestly thought I was safe because I had really good rapport with the family. My boss's boss was the CFO, and he had asked me to work on a special project analyzing some of the various business units and what it would cost to dispose of them. He told me not to read anything into that. "Don't worry about things," he said.

Two days after I finished the project, he came to my office with the VP of HR to let me know I was being laid off. I was extremely upset, not because I was losing a job, but because of the underhandedness of it. I would rather that they had been straight up with me. It wasn't like I would just walk out if I had known in advance that my position would be eliminated. I would have stuck around as long as they needed me to help with the transition. Instead, they brought the severance package down with check in hand and told me to go home. Now. I was supposed to call the VP of HR to schedule a time after hours to come back and get my stuff.

About a hundred people got laid off in a two-week span. I was one of seven to be laid off that day.

I was very angry, extremely bitter. The anger subsided in a day or two. The bitterness took a little longer. But the bottom line was that I was the only nonfamily member at this level, and family members don't get laid off. Still it was a huge blow to my ego.

I thought I'd work for this company for the rest of my life. I believed that good work would give me job security. As long as I do really good work, why would a company let me go? Even though I knew trouble was on the way, I thought I was in a good position because I had multiple talents and had worked for every operation there. If you're going to shrink your workforce, you'd think you would keep people who can do multiple things.

It took me a while to recover my confidence, but I didn't have the luxury of wallowing. I'm responsible for alimony and child support, so that was extra stressful. I gave myself two days of soul searching and grieving to get my head clear and start looking for a job.

Fortunately, I have a healthy, friendly relationship with my exwife. We transferred the kids' health insurance over to her employer's insurance, and I added the equivalent of the premiums to my child support payment.

One of the other family members from my company found out that I had been laid off and was really upset to hear the news. She offered to introduce me to someone she knew in another company who was hiring. It was perfect timing. So now I'm in a systems analyst role for a Fortune 500 company that's headquartered near me. The pay is slightly less, but the benefits are better and the long-term opportunities are better.

I hope I can get comfortable again, but never to the degree I was before. I keep my resumé up-to-date now. I'm not actively looking for a job, and if things continue to go well, I don't know that I would actively look for another job. But I won't ever be completely oblivious to what's going on.

The best thing you can do:
Be prepared. Make sure your resumé is up-to-date and maintain your business contacts. Make sure you know what's out there in the job market.

The worst thing you can do:
Wallow in self-pity. You have to get your mind set and clear as quickly as possible to look for another job. Once I started interviewing, I started feeling good about myself.

The first thing you should do:
Seek counseling so that you're mentally and emotionally focused to do what you have to do to find another job.

I've been laid off twice. The first time happened two years after I had left a great company to work for a smaller organization that offered me more growth potential. Before I took that job, I researched the company to see whether their vision, mission, and values aligned with mine. I found out they didn't even exist for the company. Part of me said, "Red flag." The other part of me said, "Opportunity to develop those things."

I was with them for about a year and a half when I started seeing signs that they were struggling. But I had survived seven rounds of layoffs at my former company, so I think I had started to feel that I was untouchable. Turned out I wasn't. It all happened rather abruptly. I got a funny feeling on a Thursday night when a meeting was canceled. And on Friday morning it was confirmed.

I can think of a few words to describe the experience, but the bottom line is that I didn't think it was handled with respect and dignity for the individual. They were very cold, very matter of fact. These were people who were not only my colleagues, but they had also become close friends over the two years I was with the company. We're still friends, and I've never asked why they handled it that way. I thought I would be the better person and let it be behind us. I choose to connect with the very positive things about my relationship with these people.

I am just like a lot of other people in American society: A lot of my self-worth is wrapped up not only in who I am but what I do. So the first time it happened to me, I felt such a sense of betrayal, and I had to work really hard to prevent what had happened to me to jade my view of humankind.

Had I not had a solid social circle and a wonderful woman in my life, I would have had a harder time. If home life and personal life is good, it helps you get through the tough times in your work life. And vice versa. When they're both good, life is grand. But when they're both not good, that's when it's really a tough time. My wife is part of my foundation, and I am very blessed to have her in my life.

It took me about six weeks between that job and starting my next job. So it was a relatively quick process. I had to root myself in the belief that everything happens for a reason. If you believe in what you do, your abilities, and you believe in who you are as a person of integrity, you have to believe that everything will find a way to work itself out. There's a greater plan.

I went through an excessive amount of emotional trauma the first time. By the time the second layoff happened to me, I had adopted this feeling that the worst thing that could happen is that I wouldn't have this job anymore. Then I could look back and say, "Well, I survived that before." I lived, and I bounced back, and I actually landed in a better place. So if that's the worst thing that could happen, I'll be okay.

When the second layoff happened to me, I knew for a number of months it could happen. I had been in a newly created role for 2 years at a place where the average length of service for salaried employees is 18 years. So when times started getting very tough in the market, I knew there was going to be a target sign painted on my back.

But that experience was completely different from my first. They were very nice to me, and my vice president continued to stay in touch with me, forwarding job postings, asking how I was doing. He really went above and beyond. I really didn't feel like I needed a tremendous amount of emotional support, but it sure was nice to know that a person was willing to offer it.

I never felt like a victim. I landed okay. I lived through it before. As long as I have a strong foundation and other aspects of my personal life is okay, I'll be fine.

The best thing you can do:
Give yourself time to think about where you are emotionally and what you want to do.

The worst thing you can do:
Give up on all your goals, objectives, dreams, and visions just because you've been laid off. Don't lose sight of the things that are most important in your life.

The first thing you should do:
Reach out to people you care about and trust and allow them to be your support mechanism. Don't isolate yourself.

PART V

LANDING YOUR NEXT JOB

CHAPTER 17

The Importance of Having a Plan

Common wisdom holds that when we suffer the death of a loved one, we shouldn't make any major life changes for six months. And common wisdom is that unexpectedly losing your job in a layoff is like suffering the death of a loved one. So it follows that when you lose your job, you shouldn't make any major life changes—like start a new job—for six months. Hmm, the logical progression falls apart right about there, doesn't it?

Unless you relish the notion of being truly and officially self-employed, languishing between jobs for six full months is intolerable and inadvisable. But the opposite extreme, leaping into the first thing that comes along, isn't such a great idea either. What would be motivating you there? Security? We already know about the illusion of the workaday world of job security now. So why leap into the fire from the frying pan just because you are pulled to the familiarity of the heat?

Bill Berman, Ph.D., Stamford, Connecticut-based corporate psychologist, says you must have a plan. And tapping away on your laptop while you're stretched out on the sofa in your PJs doesn't qualify as a plan. Neither does joyfully leaping into the arms of the first job offer that's extended to you. Borrowing from the disciplines of the corporate world (really, they do some things right), Berman suggests that you engage in what he calls personal strategic planning, to keep you on track, focused, and going after exactly what you want—and strong enough to say "no" to the wrong offers. This approach, he says, will also help keep peace in the house as you and your spouse struggle valiantly to not take your anxieties out on each other. (More about that later.)

Take some time to stop. Figure out where you stand, how much time you have to explore possibilities, what you love, and where you really want to go next. "The worst thing you can do when you get laid off is run right out and grab whatever you can," he says. "Step back and think about what you want to do, what you loved about the work you were doing before and how it matches with what you want to be doing one year, three years, five years from now."

You've probably had these questions in your mind at different times in your life. But if you've been on the all-absorbing fast track in recent years, you may have been reluctant to refresh that inquiry in your mind (even if you did have the time to think it over): "People should absolutely look at this time in their lives as an opportunity. When they're working, they try not to ask themselves, 'is this where I want to be?' That's a frightening question, especially when your life, obligations, plans and routines are built around your job. What happens if the answer is no?

"This is actually a good time to think about what you love, who you want to be, where you want to be. Is this an opportunity to be doing something different, or is this an opportunity for you to continue what you've been doing?"

Build your network list and start using it. We'll be going more deeply into networking in following chapters. But for now, it's time to start warming up to the concept of networking, which to my mind has always had the smack of soulless, overly upbeat business card swaps at Chamber of Commerce mixers. Still, networking must be done. "You are much more likely to find jobs through your relationships than through newspapers and websites," he says.

"You need to think broadly about who you know," says Berman. "Think back to the people you worked with 5, 10, 15 years ago, and don't email them. There's no substitute for a phone call."

Berman says to be upfront about telling people you're looking for a job. But don't limit your networking just to people you think might be able to directly help you land your next job. That kind of has the feeling of a booty call, doesn't it? Be genuinely interested in what's going on with the people you're talking to. Listen to what their needs are and who they are looking for in their organizations. It might not be a match for you, but you might know of just the right former coworker who was also laid off who would be a great match.

Get dressed, damn it! Treat your job search project as you would a regular full-time job. Get out of the jammies and put on something you would wear to work at your old job (assuming, of course, that you weren't fired for slovenliness). Shave, if you are a man. Come to think of it, shave, even if you are a woman. Now is not the time to explore your quirky bohemian side, unless, that's the direction you've decided to go to for your next life phase.

When you wear the uniform of your role, you stay in touch with that side of who you are. No one I can think of is in the market to hire Mr. Scratchy Pajama Bottoms. (People can tell what you're wearing—or not—by the way you sound on the phone.)

Set regular working hours that match a conventional workday. Any self-employed person will tell you that being captain of one's own hours is a joy and a curse. You have the luxury of not working when everyone else is. But then, you'll probably find yourself working when everyone else is playing. "If you work 9 to 5 on your job hunting assignment, then absolutely you can take the weekends off," says Berman. "The reason why people work on weekends and at night on looking for a new job is because they screwed around all day."

Establish a structure against which you'll achieve and measure your goals. Identify three to four core ways you'll approach your job search. How many tasks will you do each day, and what, specifically, are they? How many calls are you going to make? How many names will you look up? How many trips to the refrigerator will you take without actually opening the door?

"If you set a goal, you're going to be able to work toward that goal," says Berman. "Set very specific goals, make them things you think you can actually do, and then make them nonnegotiable."

Protect your emotional and physical health. You already know this stuff. Now you can't use a busy work schedule to be your excuse for not eating healthily or exercising the way you should. Fresh fruits and vegetables—preferably shoved through a juicer (a good way to spend your severance check, in my personal opinion)—vitamin supplements; try to stay away from sugar and stress hormone-inducing substances (which means coffee, by the way).

Negate your negative self-talk. Berman says that negative self-talk usually comes in three major self-questioning messages: Can I do it? Am I likely to do it? If I do it, will it lead to an impact? "These are questions that are always going on in the back of your consciousness; you are barely aware that they're there," says Berman. "And they have a ring of truth to them that they would never have if you say them aloud. So bring them forward from the back of your mind and say them. Then ask yourself (out loud, of course), is that true? Don't worry that someone will hear you. No one's at home; you're alone. Who's going to care?

Dismiss the derailers. Berman says that negative self-talk is only one of the influences that could derail your job search plan. That resurgence of panic that *you have to have a job now!* is a derailer. Mean-spirited friends and family who undermine your confidence with carefully placed cherry bombs (just big enough to make a mess, not big enough to cause reportable damage); well-meaning friends and family members who really, truly are concerned—especially about the passage of time; your own ego that is telling you that if you were truly a good provider, you'd have a job by now. That sort of thing. You might not be able to see them coming, but at least you can spot them for what they are. And shrug them off. Some people mean well, some people are just, well, mean. Either way, that's not your focus right now.

Partner up with your partner. If you're married or in a significant relationship, bring your partner into the plan. Two heads are better than one, of course. And, equally important, you will keep things calm at home. "Typically where fights come from during this time is that one partner is really feeling, 'I don't know what you're doing and I want to be a part of it,'" says Berman. "Use your spouse as a partner. Where you can get into trouble is where you say 'leave me alone, I can do this myself. I don't want your input.'"

"Have a plan." That seems so self-evident, doesn't it? Well, evidently, it's not. It's sort of like dieting and exercise. Everyone knows how important they are. But if we all did what we knew was best, there would be no obesity epidemic. So. Really. *Have* a plan. And then stick to it. Think of it this way: At the very least you'll get weekends off!

The best thing you can do:
Create a clear plan of what you're going to do, when you're going to do it, and how you're going to do it.

The worst thing you can do:
Take the first job you are offered because you are offered the job.

The first thing you should do:
Take a deep breath, step back, and view this as a problem to be solved by your team, which includes your family, friends, and network.

CHAPTER 18

Learn to Love Networking

About ten years ago, I gave a speech in Philadelphia to the annual conference of the Association for Women in Communications about the importance of loving your work. That was the year the folding stage collapsed under the keynoter, Jane Pauley, causing her and a 90-year-old woman to fall in a heap on top of each other. (The stage just couldn't take the shifting weight of 75 women who had politely lined up for her autograph over the previous 20 minutes.) After making sure the elderly lady—who was last in line—was okay, Pauley gamely cracked that they had all just missed the photo-op of the year. There were plenty of personal point-and-shoot cameras in the room, to be sure. But they were all kept discreetly tucked in pockets and purses as security and first aid scrambled to take care of the two grounded women.

I also remember Deborah (Bo) Sullivan, the woman who sat to my right at the luncheon right after my own speech. Over the endive salad, she told me all about the drugging problems with the Tour de France. I had sat down at that lunch not knowing— or caring—about performance drugs in sports. By the time the dessert came, I was riveted. And so for the past 10 years, every time Tour de France season rolls around, I think of Bo. We've seen each other exactly once in the intervening decade—when she and a friend of hers visited me during a summer thunderstorm while I was living in Annapolis (which is three addresses ago). And we exchange emails every now and then. That's it.

But, for some reason, her name crossed my mind when this book project crossed my desk. My challenge was to find a broad selection of people who have been laid off, who landed well, and who were willing to tell me their stories. And I needed to do it fast. Personally, I didn't know anyone who fits that description. So I had to reach out to my network. "Bo would know!" said my brain right off the bat. But it had been so long since we had exchanged emails that I had to go rooting through my ancient AOL archives just to dig up her email address. I asked her to forgive me for my being so silent only to pop up now with a request for a really important favor. And, within two days, she came through with at least five people who would be willing to talk to me—a perfect stranger—about a most painful time in their lives, just because it was she who was doing the asking. And they didn't even have to know her personally to be willing to play ball.*

"How do you know Bo?" I asked one interviewee. "I don't," she said. "We're members of the same alumni group and helping each other out is just what we do."

Networking is actually a very, very cool thing. And it's like the proverbial box of chocolates: Variety makes the selection so much better, and you just never know which piece is going to come through for you. And the flip side of this principle is that it feels really good to be the one people know they can turn to for just the right connection and introduction. Even if you're laid off and telling yourself that you're flat broke in every possible way in life, your network remains your horn of plenty, not only for yourself but also for every single person you know who could use *your* help in making important progress in *their* lives. (This is an essential point to remember. As the way we get things done is built more and more on open-source relationship building, you've got to be willing to pony up your peeps. To have the reputation of being someone who is stingy with the Rolodex could be as much a career killer as having a rap sheet.)

---

* One good turn deserves at least another. And so in the spirit of networking, allow me to turn your attention to Bo's fantastic sports blog: www.thesportsdiva.com.

If you're like me, you may have grown up loathing the notion of networking. When I hear that word I always conjure up the image of a cheesy business mixer with everyone's pockets bulging with a bundle of business cards—their own. Behind their bright smiles, they're really more interested in handing their cards out, without much interest in filling the other pocket with other people's cards. That scenario just reeks of inauthenticity: Everybody's talking, no one's listening.

Now you're out of work, or on the brink of being, shall we say, "presently at liberty." Your neediness makes it even worse to reach out to people—especially those you haven't spoken to for, like, ages.

"You know what? They haven't reached out to you either," says Donna Fisher, a Houston-based consultant and author of *Power Networking*, who specializes in training people to network effectively. "Somebody's got to be the first one to reach out. It might as well be you. Who knows? They could be out of work, too, and you will know just the right person for them to meet.

"Networking is simply a process for people to help one another, that's what we're here for," she says. "If everybody who is out of work was out there networking for everyone else who is out of work, everybody would get back to work more quickly."

Don't be shy to reach out. Fisher says that people want to help, especially these days when everyone has either been laid off or knows someone who has been laid off. And so coast to coast— maybe even around the world, given the fact this is one big global economy—people understand that this is an era of no-fault layoffs. And even if they haven't met you in person, or haven't seen you in a decade, it will make them feel good to help you. See? So you're actually doing them a favor.

Expand your ideas of who might be in your network. When you're staring into the headlights of oncoming joblessless, it's easy to come up with "no one" as you start thinking about who might be able to help you on your job search. You think back on the past five years or so and can't recall a single name of anyone who is in your life outside of your immediate family (and some of those folks you're not so sure about). Give yourself some time, a pen, and a lot of paper. Okay, now that you have beaten yourself up for having lived such an unbalanced life in recent years, who *really* do you know? People you went to school with. Your former company's customers. Your vendors (who will want to be very nice to you because you will be in the position to buy from them again one day; they're networking too, you know). People you worship with. Your kids' friends' parents. The people who work in the office suite next to yours. (No kidding, I once actually successfully interviewed for a job with the organization in the office next door when I ran into the hiring manager in the ladies room. Our commonality other than the obvious ladies room thing? We were each checking our rear views in the mirror to make sure our skirts weren't tucked into our respective panty hose. We talked things over; we made an appointment for a more formal interview at a more suitable location. And then she offered me a job. See? You just never know).

Be genuinely curious about the people you're reaching out to. This isn't just about you, you know. Find out what they've been up to. Be happy for them when they tell you about having met their major life's goals. Find out what's next on their to-do lists (by which I don't mean, shopping for grapefruit, but perhaps getting their child into the college you graduated from). And start wracking your brains to think of introductions you can make for them that will move them along toward their next dreams.

Be specific about the help you need. Fisher says not to just hand out resumés and not actually articulate what you want. If you hand someone your resumé, you're giving them something to do, which, more often than not, is to lose it. Accidentally on purpose. After you tell them what you're looking for, ask them for specific ideas of who they know who might be able to push you along the way toward your goals. "Engage my brain," says Fisher. "And then, when you follow up on my suggestion, email me or call me to let me know that you've taken that step. That engages my brain again, and I'll start thinking about what else I can do for you."

Remember those thank-you notes. Even better, buy a box of elegant notecards, because you should be using them up with all the networking that you're going to be doing. Everyone who is helping you along the way deserves a handwritten note with a special message just for them so that they know how much you value having them in your network. And, oh by the way, any time you can help them, just say the word.

> **The best thing you can do:**
> Keep in mind that you're a valuable connection in other people's networks.
>
> **The worst thing you can do:**
> Pass out your resume with no effort to make a sincere, personal connection with the person whose help you want.
>
> **The first thing you should do:**
> Make a list of at least 101 people you know. You may hit a wall at number 35, but keep going anyway. Your brain will get the idea and start cooperating.

CHAPTER 19

Using Social Networking for Your Job Search

There's this guy out there who likes to make you think that maybe you know him. He sends out invitations to join his network via LinkedIn.com, which is really supposed to be only for people who know each other. But, nevertheless, you may get an email from him with a personal invitation. "Hmmm," you think. "The name doesn't ring a bell. But, we're all getting older, memory's not what it used to be, meeting more and more people. Maybe we met at a conference. I'll just click on the invitation link, and maybe I'll remember him after I read further."

Now he's got you. Very quickly, in a box that's supposed to be reserved for a personal message between two friends, he launches into an obvious cut-and-paste description of his business, his services, and what he can do for you. And to make it worse, the services he offers have nothing to do with anything you could ever possibly want in this lifetime. Not interested? No biggie, he says, magnanimously (how big of him). "Just archive me," he graciously suggests. But that won't do you any good. By clicking Archive you're just leaving your door open so that he can walk right through it at a later date.

You haven't even officially let him into your personal sphere of influence, and he still managed to slime you with a pitch. This is not the way to use social networking. Play nice, follow community rules, and social networking can open up surprising opportunities for you. You just need to know how to work the system to your best advantage and to stand out from the crowds of many milling networkers all wanting to keep each other up-to-date on their doings, which can be as trivial as adventures in plate painting and new puppy antics. Still, it's also a great way to get a job that's perfect for you.

Online social networking is a fantastic way to circulate the word about yourself, your abilities, and your availability, says Patrice-Anne Rutledge, author of *The Truth About Profiting from Social Networking*. "This is Job Search 2.0," she says, "and it is a much more robust way to build your career than just relying on the more traditional ways of printing out your resumés and net-working."

By using the tools and techniques available to you on these sites, she says, you have much more control over your job-search activities, even if part of your strategy is to be a so-called *passive* seeker, letting recruiters come to you. And they will, if you play your cards right. Recruiters know from firsthand experience that finding the proverbial needle in the proverbial haystack is much faster and more efficient if they search online than if they tackle the stack of unsolicited resumés that come to them via snail mail. Additionally, they know that anyone who is savvy enough to build a spot-on online presence is current with the cutting-edge career-building technologies. And that tells them that at least you've been paying attention over the past five years or so.

Understand the difference among the major social network-ing sites, and which ones are most conducive to job search-ing. LinkedIn.com is best known for people who want to keep their best business foot forward. Rutledge says that more than 100,000 recruiters also have their own profiles posted on LinkedIn. So that's one big, active marketplace filled with peo-ple who want to do business. While it positions itself as a Euro-pean market leader, Xing.com has a decidedly global flavor in that it brags about having 6.5 million business professionals all over the world, with posted networking events from Brussels to Sydney to Dubai to Beijing to Athens to Berlin, and so on. There are many other sites, and you don't have to restrict yourself to just one. Just bear in mind that your presence on certain sites, like these two, will position yourself as someone who takes his or her career extremely seriously.

Create your online profile with recruiters in mind. Let's start with the easy part first: your photo. Make it a respectable business photo that's relatively current. And make it a picture of *you*. (I confess that on one of the sites I'm active on, my photo—or avatar—is of my three cats, which I hear, is one of those indications that I might be on my way to being a crazy lady. But I'm not looking for a job; you are.) No cats, no dogs, no baby pictures. There's one picture I have personally seen of a guy strategically positioned directly behind a gigantic, shall we say, appendage, that's at least 6 feet long. That is just not a good idea. Even if he's not looking for a job. He might be looking for a girlfriend. Oh. Maybe he is.

As for the rest of your profile, think of it as an electronic document with tons of buttons on it. Each button is an opportunity for recruiters to find you. And so each button should be a keyword that is directly pertinent to how marvelous you are as a professional. Your education, your certifications, the companies you've worked for, the projects you've completed, the products that you use on the job. Where you live. Where you want to live. Think of everything that is true about you that would make a recruiter's eyes light up. And then think of how you can make your profile go "Ding! Ding! Ding! Ding! Ding!" with all those lit buttons. And now you have the makings of a profile that is a compelling recruiter magnet. Use those keywords to your advantage.

Scour these sites' online job marketplaces. You're also an *active* job seeker. And these sites are only going to get better and better as years move along and recruiters increasingly use them. LinkedIn has made its marketplace so much better to use than the traditional online lists of job postings in that it also indicates for you whether you have a person in your network who might know someone personally in the company that's posting the job. This way you don't have to join the throng of resumé pitchers who are applying for those jobs. You can use your network exactly the way you should, which is to see whether you can snag yourself a personal introduction to someone on the inside who will make the hiring decision.

Work the system; don't try to beat it. Good social networking citizens know that their communities will stay civilized only if everyone minds their manners. If you try to sleaze your way into a harmonious group of openly sharing people, you'll be as welcome (not to mention as obvious) as a lounge lizard at an anniversary party. I know that wouldn't be you. But I bet you can think of a friend or two you can give this advice to.

Have fun on vacation but know your limits. Remember that what goes on the Web stays on the Web. So leave your digital camera in your room if you already know in advance that, with just one margarita, you are likely to lift—or drop—an article of clothing that back home normally remains held properly in place. Ditto the photos of your tattoos. Don't count on the hope that your buttoned-up LinkedIn presence will be all that recruiters see. They'll check out Facebook and MySpace, as well, which seem to be where the really gross pictures (like the previously mentioned one) end up.

Get involved in as many social networking groups as you have time for. Spend some time searching the thousands of special-interest groups that these sites play host to. Your high school alum, for starters. People who like to scuba dive on sunken school buses in flooded Midwest quarries, maybe. Fans of Mr. Green Jeans. Fans of Mr. Moose. People who think that Bunny Rabbit had a criminal mind. You'll be amazed at who's out there and who welcomes people just like them to chat and compare notes. It's actually scary, when you think about it. This world has got to get back to work. (Just make sure that whatever groups you get caught up in will lead you to the kinds of jobs you want. These things can take up a lot of time and attention. And it won't look so good if recruiters Google your name—they will—and Google brings up a predominance of hits of you weighing in on the Bunny Rabbit controversy. Recruiters aren't especially attracted to candidates with a lot of demonstrable time on their hands.)

I'm aware of the fact that social networking is evolving so fast that almost anything I could write about it now (except for the preceding pieces of advice) will be improved upon by the time this book lands in your hands. And that's very good news because that means the world has become an even better place to find work that's good enough for you.

The best thing you can do:
If you're new to social networking, set aside a half day, make yourself very comfortable in front of the computer (you can even wear your pajamas for this project), and just explore the world of social networking sites.

The worst thing you can do:
Do things online that you wouldn't do in front of a boss in person.

The first thing you should do:
Enjoy the exploration.

CHAPTER 20

Build Your "A" Player Status Even Though You Are Not Employed

You might be out of a job but don't think you're necessarily out of work. You can even be making money during this downtime. As a knowledge worker, your toolkit remains in your head—it's not like you had to turn it back into the company at your last punch-out. And, because almost all of us have some sort of computer access, you have everything you need to continue building your visibility and even prestige while you're waiting for the employment side of things to turn around for you.

In fact, ironically enough, now that you're a free agent, this is your chance to hit major professional goals for yourself. Your time is your own, and you don't need anyone's permission to step right up and reach up a little higher than you could when you were embedded inside a team that was bound by politics, egos, and layers of authority that you had to kowtow to.

When companies begin hiring again (in fact, someone could be considering you right now), they're going to wonder what you've been doing with your brain during these months when you've been on your own. The projects that you undertake right now, the thought leadership that you drive while you're on your own will far outweigh any old, outdated handicap that you might have felt that kept you from "A" player status before (like the pedigree of your college degree, for instance).

This is your chance to build new relationships and rack up the successful completion of projects. This is your chance to stand out from the crowd and have great stories to tell of your adventures as a free agent.

Be a Thought Leader

Keep up with your industry and keep your opinions coming. You have a lot to share, and the value of your perspective hasn't changed simply because your title has. Renew your professional memberships and create presentations that you can deliver to your local chapters (as well as the chapters in other regions where you might like to build awareness of who you are). Write articles for your chapter newsletters. Make yourself available to mentor newcomers to your profession.

Be Googlable

If you have a gmail.com or aol.com or yahoo.com address, I have only one question for you: *What are you thinking?* Domain names are so cheap these days—not to mention even Web design services—you should have your name as your domain name at the very least. I'm sorry if your name is John Smith— that name might be already taken. But surely there's something that you can figure out so that you can create an online identity for yourself that is yours and yours alone. Sure, the free email addresses are free, but they're costing you big in terms of your public image as someone who takes him- or herself seriously.

Be Expansive

Once you have your domain name, get a Web page and put it to good use. At the very least, have your resumé posted online as a Web page. And make sure your resumé is tagged with all the keywords any recruiter would use to search for someone just like you, with your talents, abilities, and background. But don't stop there. Start building out your Web site with professional events calendars, book reviews, commentaries on professional developments, white papers. Start a blog. (Blogs are free.) Make it smart and original. Maybe even make it a little controversial. Start a conversational bonfire (just a little one, and nothing actionable against your former employer, for instance) and invite your readers to get in on the action. Be nervy enough to ask some especially prickly questions in your profession and stand back to watch the comments fly. Weigh in on other peoples' blogs as much as you can. And post a great, professional headshot of you wherever your professional persona appears—on your own site, as a regular on other peoples' sites, in online communities.

Be Opinionated
Be informed, certainly, but have a consistent point of view that people associate with you.

Be Generous with Your Connections
One of the advantages of being a free agent is that you have the freedom to build your network like you never have before. You're going to be meeting new people everywhere, and pretty soon you'll start thinking about how certain people would benefit from knowing certain other people. Start putting them together. There's a weird sense of power and satisfaction that comes from knowing that you're the one who introduced these people. That's a largesse that costs you absolutely nothing, and the ROI (return on introductions) is immeasurable.

Be Generous with Your Talents and Skills
It would be nice to actually get paid for what you do and know. But there are plenty of people and organizations who can't afford your professional services and desperately need you. Isn't it nice to feel needed? Not to mention appreciated—especially by causes you care deeply about. True, most nonprofits of any significant size have their own paid staff, and I'm not suggesting you take jobs away from these people. But you can certainly augment what they're doing with additional time and expertise. Or perhaps you can teach them the latest techniques that you picked up in the corporate world. Take on projects that you can lead from start to finish, and then publish reports on what the group accomplished on your Web site.

Be a Consultant

Even though you have absolutely no intention of starting your own business now that you're a free agent, some of your colleagues may be cultivating those dreams of independence. Good for them! They're going to need your expertise to get off the ground. They may or may not be able to actually pay you, but surely you have the time, interest, and bandwidth to lend these dreamers and help them achieve their next goals. It will help you remember your value and keep you away from the remote control and the refrigerator.

Remember That Your Former Employer Might Also Value Your Skills and Abilities

The work still has to get done, and they might be able to actually pay you more by the hour on a contract basis than they would have been able to when you were just overhead. You don't have to be a consultant forever. It's just for now.

Be Curious

If you're a knowledge professional, you're going to want to keep growing your knowledge. And you're going to want to make sure others know you're committed to growing your knowledge—and growing your profession's body of knowledge at the same time. What burning professional questions could you research the answers to and write white papers about? Which of these questions would be most likely to give you a good reason to contact your peers inside "A" player organizations as part of the research process? Which conferences would be thrilled to feature you as a presenter of your breakthrough findings?

Be Willing to Be a "B" Player

Many employers are discovering that some of the so-called "A" players aren't all they are cracked up to be. The superstars may be just meteoring through the workplace, not lasting long enough in any one position to really contribute significant value on a lasting basis before blasting on to the next high-profile, better-paying job. Because employers are looking for some stability themselves (it's not like they've been enjoying these hair-trigger times, either, you know), they're going to want to hire people they can depend on. Recruiting and retaining is still expensive. So a modest, steady-Eddy posture could be the very thing that makes you stand out from the crowd of crowing preeners.

Be There

Get out of the house. By which I mean, go to professional meetings, conferences, and lectures. Going to the supermarket doesn't count (but, as long as you stay out of the candy and beer aisles, it couldn't hurt). Go to where the smart people are and hang out after the event is over. Mingle at receptions, talk about what you're doing. (Hedge trimming the poodle is off limits, though; try to keep it professional.) Get people's business cards; make sure they get yours.

The best thing you can do:
Assign yourself a research project, and then build up a list of all the people you would like to encourage to work with you on it.

The worst thing you can do:
Convince yourself that you're no one without a company title.

The first thing you should do:
Remind yourself that you may have lost your job, but you haven't lost your reason for being.

CHAPTER 21

Talking About Your Job Loss in Interviews

Any successful salesperson will tell you that if you don't believe in the product you're pitching, you might as well pack it in. With that in mind, how easy do you think it's going to be to present yourself to the employment marketplace when the last thing you heard from your employer was something along these lines:

"You know what? We don't want you *so badly* that we're actually willing to pay you *this much money* just to beat it." Whether your severance check is puny or spectacular, it's hard not to take a layoff like a clop across the chops. And then how can you possibly present damaged goods to the marketplace that you would want to work in?

Duncan Mathison, a San Diego-based director of executive coaching for a global outplacement firm, has a great solution for counteracting the gravitational pull of the downer career narrative. Have yourself a really great story. Tell the truth, of course. But you can still keep it upbeat and use your experience to showcase your strengths.

And when you have your story created according to Mathison, you will be ready to go back out into the market, searching for the next right position, with the confidence that you deserve and have earned in your years as a high performer.

Crafting your story may take more than a few drafts, he says, but it can be done. And when you do it right (finally), you'll be able to position yourself in a positive light that sets you apart from all those overly bright, howdy-howdy candidates who are hoping that their happy behavior will mask the pain they're feeling inside. It won't.

For starters, says Mathison, "It's important to come to terms with two important things: why you were released, and how you can talk about it in a positive way." The story should only take two minutes. (Really. Mathison times it with his clients.) And by the time you're done, you will have positioned yourself as the perfectly passionate professional who totally gets the hard realities of tough business decisions. No hard feelings. See? You're so ready to get back to work and find a place that is a great fit for your skills and values.

"The discipline in keeping it to two minutes is really essential," says Mathison. "It's about bandwidth and some control of the conversation. You want to be able to tell them the whole story while you have the floor, but by two minutes they will have started thinking of questions that they want to ask you. Keep your story to two minutes, and control the way you end the story, and you'll be able to control the way the conversation goes from there."

Here's how the story breaks down: The first five to ten seconds should be some sort of headline summation of who you are. Mathison says that it's important to find that nugget piece of information that captures the overriding theme of your career or what motivates you. Start with a sentence such as this: "Throughout my career, I've always been fascinated by _____." In my case, I would say, "I've dedicated my career to exploring ways that people achieve their potential and express their passion inside the world of work."

Now you try.

Once you have that down, you go into the story of your career, tracking each job (starting from your school years, if there's an interesting or relevant story to tell), why you chose each position, what you learned with each one, and how others decided it was time for you to take the next spot. Be sure to mention the fact that your progression was energized by other people noticing your value and choosing you. Remember that this isn't just a read-through of your resumé. This is a story with consistent, underlying themes that support your opening narrative.

"What you're telling about yourself when you track through your entire career in this way is what motivates you, what your values are, that you were paying attention enough to know that you were on an ongoing learning track, what exactly you were learning, and that other people around you recognized your performance and kept selecting you for promotions or projects," says Mathison.

Eventually, of course, you'll come to the end. And this is where your story gets good. Assuming you've been truly laid off, you have nothing to be ashamed of. And you certainly don't want to position yourself as someone who is harboring a grudge against your former employer (even though you might be, just a little bit). You want to position yourself in the minds of the people you're talking to as someone who is a reasoned, seasoned, and stable partner in the business of business.

So here it goes from here: "As you know, there have been a lot of pressures on our industry lately, especially with this economy. The company did what it really needed to do, which was to let a lot of really great people go. And so now I'm currently in the market for _____." And then fill in the blank, making sure that what you say you're looking for is a position to help *them,* not make your own dreams come true. Know what I mean?

Concluding your story this way tells them very specific things: You completely understand the harsh but unfortunate realities of business. You don't hold a grudge. And that you were one of those really great people who were let go. The logic goes this way: You were let go, clearly. They let go really great people. Therefore you must be a really great person. And you can say all that without actually coming right out and saying it. Let them draw their own conclusions.

But you're not quite done yet. One more step to go.

"You follow up your story by asking them a question about themselves," says Mathison.

"Tell me a little bit about your organization."

Or "How is your organization addressing these shifts in the marketplace?"

Not: "Enough about me, let's talk about you. What questions do you have for me?"

Mathison warns that if you invite your interviewee to start asking questions about you, he or she is going to go straight to the most immediately recent topic, which is how you lost your job. You don't want that. You want to go in a different direction.

"You want to drive the conversation forward around the agenda you want them to disclose to you," says Mathison, meaning: what's important to them in their business, what they are looking for, who else they know who might be looking for someone just like you. That sort of thing.

If you continue to be worried that your bruises of self-doubt are still showing through your confidence, Mathison has this perspective to share with you: "Remember that the only thing that makes a manager really successful is the ability to meet and hire really great people," he says. "And you're the right person for a number of managers out there.

"If you can help a manager find the right person, and that person is you, you're doing that manager a huge favor."

The best thing you can do:
Assume that there are a number of opportunities for you out there. Your job is to find them because they're not going to find you.

The worst thing you can do:
Go out into the job market when you're still emotionally raw from the layoff experience.

The first thing you should do:
Create a list of every organization that might be a potential employer. Your mission right now isn't about finding jobs. It's about finding people who hire people like you.

CHAPTER 22

How to Evaluate the Job You've Been Offered

Setting aside the not-inconsequential issue of money for just a moment, it's essential to remember that so much more goes into deciding whether a new potential employer is the one for you. In Chapter 24, "Go! Just Say Yes," we go into the fine points of negotiating in today's economy. (Hint: It's a short chapter.) But for now, let's make sure you know how to tell whether the company is a good fit for you, or just an invitation to be unemployed again before you've had time to program your new cell phone. Bearing in mind that nothing's permanent (or even guaranteed) in the grand career scheme of things, you also want to know that your next selection is a reasonably logical choice on your own professional progression. Or at the very least, you should be able to get a whole new set of really great stories to tell, for the next time you have to fashion your two-minute story.

In my own personal employment history, I've trended toward the "hot diggity dog, I got myself a job!" approach to discerning my job options. But the brainiacs among the industrial and organizational psychology crowd frown on such, shall we say, emotion-based methodology. Like Jeffrey Saltzman, a principal at Kenexa—a global talent management firm, which has probably already seen your resumé, if you have ever submitted an online application anywhere. Predictably (oh, how I do love the way his mind works), he suggests that you use a framework—in this case, a four-box confidence grid—to analyze a prospective employer and what it might have to offer you.

	Internal	External
Organizational Confidence		
Personal Confidence		

"When you use a framework," says Saltzman, "You are going to make better judgments. The framework is extremely useful and powerful in helping people get their thoughts around potential employers and their attractiveness.

"Companies use comparison tools to evaluate the desirability of each candidate over the others. Why shouldn't individuals use the same tools to consider the desirability of a potential employer?" says Saltzman. Personally, my evaluation techniques have been primarily based on variations of "I'm going out for a walk." And Plan B, which I rarely use, has routinely been, "Let me sleep on it."

Saltzman counters with, "Any time you can take a step back, pull the emotion out of the decision and look at things in a more rational way, you will make better decisions."

Let's consider his grid, shall we?

Organizational Confidence/Internal
What do you know about the way the organization is run, and who's running it? What are its mission, vision, and values, and does its actions reflect its intangibles put into action? Does the management appear to understand the value of high-quality talent and the importance of providing professional development? When you talk to these people, can they articulate exactly how your job fits into the company's mission? Are they willing to help you understand what success looks like vis à vis your performance and how it will be measured? Are they going to give you the tools you need to actually do your job? (Some of these

considerations sound very closely related to the questions on engagement surveys you've filled out in the past, don't they? It's interesting how engagement is still essential, even in these times. Only now it's you who's doing the asking.)

Speaking of employee engagement…You know those wonderful Best Employer lists that come out every year. Personally I adore them. It's like the old Sears Wish Book that came out every holiday season when I was a kid. But my advice to you is to take them with a grain of salt. The people who put those lists together bend over backward to make sure they're built with unimpeachable data and metrics. But many companies that compete for spaces on those lists hire communications services that make it their business to outsmart the system. (I'm not saying who…but I could.)

Organizational Confidence/External
Put on your investor hat and consider the company's viability as an enterprise. How well is the company positioned in its industry sector? Does it have strong products and services? Is it a tough competitor, setting the standard against which everyone else falls all over themselves to copy? How does its stock compare to others in its industry? Right now all stocks have been taking a beating. So, if the company's stock price is staying with its industry sector pack, that's at least a neutral sign. And maybe neutral is as good as it gets for a while. If you spot a wholesale sell-off of company stock in an industry sector that's at least holding tight on life support, however, you can assume that the analysts and big-volume buyers might know something you don't .

Personal Confidence/Internal
If you took a job with this particular company, what would your career look like inside the organization? Does it attract the best and brightest of your profession so that you are constantly

growing and learning just by teaming up with these people? Will you be able to shine your own light brightly in the company of a confident bunch? Or do you suspect that you might have to hide your light under the proverbial bushel just to get along?

"When I'm surrounded by mediocrity, it's a depressing situation," says Saltzman. You probably recognize the feeling. Don't you? Thought so.

Are you confident that this organization is committed to coaching, mentoring, and career development for people in your function or at your professional level? Or is this an organization that's hiring for an immediate need? And if that need were to go away, would you be back on the layoff list? And, if that were to be the case, would that be okay with you?

Personal Confidence/External

If you had a perceptive (or buttinsky) mom, you probably heard the expression, "Show me your friends, and I'll show you your future." Same principle goes with employers. Chances are that this prospective employer won't be your last. So, will this be a good company to be *from?* We can all think of certain companies whose cachet associated with its management quality or innovation or humanitarianism will help doors fling wide open for their alum as they roam the great wide world. Google. Apple. Microsoft. Genentech. Patagonia. Pepsi. How long do you think their former employees would be allowed to remain on the loose before they're snatched up? So as you're considering whether this employer is an attractive option to you, you should also consider whether future employers will find you attractive for having spent time there.

Saltzman also points out that there's a virtual circle associated with working for a high-prestige company: The more desirable the company is, the more desirable you will be to its competitors; therefore, the more your company could want to hang on to you because it's far better that it should keep your talent to itself. Follow?

Don't throw away Saltzman's grid once you have said yes to your company of choice. Things change, you know. Just as your employer conducts (or should conduct) a regular review with you on your performance and goals, you do the same. Take out that grid every few months or so and consider how it's holding up to your actual experiences of the company. How is its performance meeting your expectations?

"When you see the grid start to fall apart," says Saltzman, "Maybe it's time to think about expanding your horizons."

The best thing you can do:
Consider your prospective employers through the same unemotional, critical eye that they're using to consider you with.

The worst thing you can do:
Leap willy-nilly at the first job offer that comes along, without regard to what it will do to your career over time.

The first thing you should do:
Find a ruler. (In a manner of speaking. I'm sure you know Word and Excel.)

CHAPTER 23

Should You Take a Job with a Company That's Laying People Off?

In economic times when job opportunities seem scarce, it's tempting to ignore your inner warning bells and leap for the first job offer that comes along. But what happens if that job offer is from a company that is actually laying off employees? How smart is it to take a job there? It could be very smart, depending on what you want, who you are, where you are in your career, and whether the company knows what it's doing. It seems counterintuitive to see job listings placed by companies that have announced massive layoffs. But there could be some excellent opportunities inside these organizations. The question is: Are those opportunities a good fit for you?

Some Good Reasons to Take the Job

- **You're just starting your career, and the company is filling its new-hire pipeline with high-potential newbies.** Some companies have the foresight to know that their future depends on grooming a wealth of early careerists who might be around for a while. You know that this company at least has the long-term perspective to believe that it will survive the current crisis and will need people just like you in the long run. That's a sign that there might be some kind of talent management plan in place. It might not be so apparent to the people boxing up the contents of their desks, but at least you can get started in your career there. Even if you do get laid off three years down the road (remember, no promises), three years at that company are better than three years saving yourself for a nonexistent promise and killing afternoons watching *Dr. Phil*.

- **The company is changing strategy, and the job you're applying for directly serves that strategy.** No matter what kind of work you want to pursue in the corporate world, you can find a company that regards your skillset as an essential piece of its revenue-generating machine. "How does this position fit your strategy moving forward?" would be a very smart question to ask the interviewer. A clear response will tell you that, for the time being, your job is relatively secure.

- **The company would look great on your resumé.** So what if it turns out you're only there for a couple of years? If the company is top notch, the training, exposure, and insights you get could be like an MBA course in an A Player graduate school.

- **You need the skills and experience that this job will give you.** Certain career paths require certain tickets to be punched. And depending on where you are in your life and career, your career path ticket may be more important than job security or the prospect of having to explain to people why you're in the job market again a few years down the road.

Signs That the Job Might Not Be the Best Choice

- **The hiring manager sends off angry or distracted vibes.** Listen to your intuition. In a company that's laying off dozens, hundreds, or thousands of people, you're going to be walking past empty desks and depressed people. That's natural. Tragic, but to be expected. However, if the person interviewing you for the job—especially if the person would be your supervisor—is giving you the impression that "this place is a pit," go with that. There are way too many stories of people quitting perfectly good jobs to take on a better-paying position elsewhere, only to find themselves canned along with the rest of their new department before they have even received their new business cards.

- **The hiring manager seems freakishly cheerful.** Who is he trying to snooker? Himself? Or you?

- **Your interviewer can't clearly paint the picture for you as to how this position directly serves the company strategy.** Can you understand and explain in one simple, easy sentence how this job is essential to the company's direction? No? Call it a day.

- **The job isn't exactly a new one, and the person you're replacing isn't exactly a young one.** Take a look around the prospective new department or company. Anyone over the age of, say, 45? No? Better find out why not. If the company itself is young or in a trendy business, like fashion or video games, perhaps there's a good reason why all the employees are young. Or perhaps the downsizing company handed out absolutely irresistible early (and totally voluntary) early-retirement packages. Check it out before making any assumptions—or talking yourself out of a gut feeling that this would be a bad choice. A company without laugh lines could be a company without integrity.

- **You need some sign of stability on your resumé.** This isn't about the company; it's about you. If you are a job hopper, and you have a track record of being in one job for only a year or so, you might want to mix it up a little bit and find a company where you can be reasonably sure that you'll be staying for a while. Happily, job hopping doesn't have the stigma it used to have, as long as you can clearly tell a story of how each position has built your skills, knowledge, growth, and maturity—all of which tells an employer good things about you. But, even in fast-moving economic times, it's smart to pepper your resumé with a little longevity every now and then. If this is the time to do that, try to make very sure that this employer won't be taking the hatchet to your department or position any time soon.

The best thing you can do:
Keep your mind open to all possible employment opportunities, until you learn more about the company's strategic plans.

The worst thing you can do:
Come to a knee-jerk "no" just because the company is known to be laying off people.

The first thing you should do:
Ask your interviewer to explain clearly to you how this open position serves the company's business objectives.

CHAPTER 24

Go! Just Say Yes

I suppose we all have memories of negotiation moments of truth that make us want to slap our foreheads, and go, "Stupid! Stupid! Stupid!" No? Well. Here's mine anyway. I was applying for my first job as a business journalist. The salary was no mystery. It was posted everywhere. And the application process involved a test to gauge my writing and editing abilities. I was the youngest of the applicants, and—I believe but couldn't swear to this in court—the only woman. What I delivered clearly set me apart from the other candidates, and I was offered the job. The only thing was this, explained my prospective managing editor, with fatherly concern in his eyes, the editorial board in their great wisdom determined that I was too young to receive such a salary. And so they felt it only right and appropriate to reduce the offer. By 25%. "You understand," he said, as though only an insane person would see the subterranean cracks in logic and fairness in the situation as he presented it.

Did I take it? Let's just say that my negotiation style was uncannily similar to Sally Field's Oscar acceptance speech when she won for *Places in the Heart*. (It's on YouTube, if you don't know it.) And to think I worked for these guys for three whole years! I'm still in touch with this editor, Christmas cards mostly. Every now and then the thought crosses my mind that I really should get some closure on this. But then I remind myself that he's an old man now, and if he's not thinking about it while riding pyramid camels at Giza, so much the better for him.

All of which is to say, I'm really not the person to go to for negotiation advice. However, Wharton Business School professor (and director of the Wharton Executive Negotiation Workshop), Richard Shell, is. He also wrote the book *Bargaining for*

Advantage: Negotiation Strategies for Reasonable People. And, as of right now, the end of 2008 when the words *recession* and *job loss* are on everyone's lips, he would agree with my tactics, such as they are.

"This is going to be a short chapter," he said to me ruefully. "Tell them to just say yes." But then he said more:

> "When the economy is going for record unemployment, you don't negotiate. You accept the offer. Then your job is to exceed expectations once you're inside the organization. Then you have a good platform to ask for raises and promotions."

I won't say that the days of signing bonuses, relo packages, and incremental negotiation strategies are completely over. But I sure wouldn't count on them right now. Reason? As the candidate you have zero leverage. And, says Shell, leverage is what it's all about when negotiating. Right now, in most industries and with most openings, you have two positions. "Yes," which is great, especially when you can start right away. Or "no," which is okay by the hiring managers, because even if you might be their first choice, there are plenty more candidates almost just as wonderful as you are who would happily say yes. Don't think these hiring managers have already identified their second, third, or fourth picks. Plus, who knows? *You* could be their third choice because Picks One and Two had the temerity to say, "Can I think about it?"

"You don't negotiate when the item you want is in scarce supply," he says. "You just say yes and remember that you're lucky to get it."

Shell says that the smartest move you can make is accept the offer now (assuming it's one that you really want) and then build your position of strength by being so gosh darn great to work with. You start building that position of strength the instant you begin the new job—starting with yourself.

"Now you have an income again, and you're repairing your self-esteem," he says. "Now you have the chance to differentiate yourself by your performance and the way you demonstrate how you can help solve people's problems. You become valuable, and maybe if you're lucky, you become indispensable. And *then* you're back in the game."

But what about leverage? Once you're inside the organization, folded into their pay and promotion schedules, don't you lose your leverage? Doesn't your choice of positions change to "Yes, right away!" and "No, I quit?" Shell says you've got much more power than that.

"Inside organizations, leverage derives from dependencies," he says. "You become indispensable when you know who needs what and you can deliver as much of it as they need. Once you start delivering things to people in a way that's value-oriented, it's going to be that much harder to replace you and put someone else in your place. If you go above and beyond the call for them, they're going to like that and want to have you around.

"With that foundation, you might have the chance to negotiate beyond the starting position you were in within the organization. Or start looking for a different job at a different company—and negotiate there—because you are starting from a stronger position of having a job already."

Shell says that effective negotiation is 90% attitude and 10% tactics. Right now, especially if you've been laid off, your attitude might have taken a beating. So it might be difficult to project an authentic, balanced air of confidence and enthusiasm. And given the state of the economy at the moment, your tactics are quite simple. Just say yes.

The best thing you can do:
Be very clear about your priorities.

The worst thing you can do:
Act out of desperation.

The first thing you should do:
Present yourself enthusiastically.

Voice of Experience: Deborah

I was working for a company that bought its largest competitor. There were three companies that did what we did, and we bought one of them. On April 1, we all met and had this big party. Then on May 1, I was called in and told I was being laid off. It turned out the corporate severance policy for the company that we acquired was very generous, and my company didn't have a severance policy at all. And it would have cost too much to let the new company's people go, so they let two-thirds of the original staff go. They just paid us for two weeks, and we were gone. In one month, we went from thinking, "This is great, we are safe, we just eliminated our biggest competitor" to "Oh my God, we're unemployed."

My first reaction was terror. But I got a two-week reprieve because I was in the middle of rolling out a new product. And having had the opportunity to stay in my normal routine for those two weeks, I was able to think things through more reasonably and logically. If I had just been sent home with my box of stuff out of my desk, I'm not sure what I would have done.

It gave me an advantage because I had access to my mailing list for those two weeks. And so I wrote a cover letter for my resumé that said, "You're familiar with the quality of my work. As we're all aware, people are displaced from their jobs through no fault of their own. I would really appreciate any help you could give me." And then I sent this letter to the full client list before I left. Everyone has a list of clients/vendors that they can work with. You can do the same thing.

I got the most wonderful responses from all different kinds of people, asking me what I wanted to do next. Two people separately sent my resumé to the same person who was doing a search. She had already decided to hire someone else, but when she read my resumé, she saw that I had been an opera singer and that I was interested in politics. And so she thought, "She's really interesting, I want to meet her." So I went to the interview, and she gave me a test to take home. I brought it back to her the next day, and she hired me on the spot.

They say your resumé should be very factual, straightforward, and dry. Every time I've gotten a job, it was because I looked like an interesting person to talk to.

I'm also basically a positive person, which helps. Nobody wants to hire a Gloomy Gus. Everyone is in a stressful situation, everyone. And so they want to bring in people who are able to make the best of stressful situations. If you come into the interview with the attitude that "this is just going to be a waste of my time," it's a waste of their time and your time. If you come in with the idea that "this is going to be the one," you go in believing that you can make a difference here. They're looking for someone who can make a difference here. Every new job opening is a search for someone who can make a difference. You may decide during the interview itself that that's not true. But then you make that decision and move on.

The best thing you can do:
It's important to build strong personal relationships with your clients and vendors. When you're displaced, the best people who can help you are not the people you worked with, but the people you worked with outside your organization. Your vendors work with people like you across the industry. Your clients know what you bring to the table in a way that nobody else does.

The worst thing you can do:
Panic.

The first thing you should do:
Know exactly what the company is offering you. Talk to someone in HR to make sure you understand what your benefits situation is so that you don't put yourself in a worse position financially by making a foolish mistake. If they offer outplacement services, use them.

CHAPTER 25

Start Your New Job with Confidence

Companies may be laying people off, but they're also hiring. And sooner or later (preferably sooner), your time will come to start a new job—hopefully within shouting distance of your former salary and management level. If you're assuming a new job with a leadership component to your duties, you've got a new set of challenges to prepare yourself for. In good times, the failure rates of newly employed leaders are abysmal. (Some say as many as 60% to 70% of newly hired managers are fired within six months of taking on their new jobs.) If you're taking on a leadership job in bad times, you know that there is a long line of candidates ready to step in if you fail. And you may think that the psychological wounds of losing your previous job might get in the way of your taking charge with confidence. Right now you have to find a way to exude confidence and assume leadership when you might be feeling the least confident and not nearly as leaderly as you might like.

Says Mark Walztoni, a Santa Fe-based executive coach who specializes in the first 100 days of a leader's new job: "New leaders are facing three emotional roadblocks when they are starting a new job, especially after they've been laid off. They know the stakes are extremely high and don't want to be in the job market again. So they become risk averse—and could ultimately get fired for being ineffective. Or they go back to old behaviors that may or may not have worked for them before, but are completely inappropriate to their new jobs. Or they completely overcompensate for their self-doubt and behave too forcefully and aggressively in their new one."

Isn't it comforting to know there are three ways you can totally screw up your new job? But you can also succeed brilliantly in your new job. You just need a plan to take things one step at a time and to ask your new coworkers (and boss) to help you succeed.

Assess your current people skills. Objectively consider your strengths and weaknesses as a manager before going into your new job. What did the 360-degree feedback reports from your last job tell you about where you shine as a leader and where you could use some coaching? How about your direct reports' engagement survey scores? Do you have a former employee who is confident enough to tell you the truth, even if it's difficult truth? The culture of your new company may be drastically different from that of your former organization. But people are pretty much the same in terms of how they like to be treated. Now, before you start your new job, is a very good time to identify those behaviors that make you a great people leader (so that you can do more of those) and those behaviors that you would benefit from correcting.

Ask your new boss to help you identify two or three critical goals you can achieve during your first three months. Walztoni characterizes them as "small enough to win, big enough to matter." What's the objective? How will success be measured? How will your boss want to be told that these goals have been reached?

Plan an initial, focused, mandatory meeting with your team to discuss work styles. Walztoni suggests that a minimum of two hours be set aside for this first meeting. Dedicate the first hour to explaining your management style, what's important to you in terms of performance, behaviors, and results.

At the second hour, throw the floor open to your new direct reports. Give them the chance to tell you how they like to work, what makes them feel good about their jobs, how they like to be recognized, what they need to feel motivated. This is the time for you to demonstrate that you're a listening leader and that you care what their input is. Show your new team that they can tell you anything, the difficult news and the positive. That you will hear it and understand it. And then take action, if necessary.

Walztoni says, "Ask them what two or three changes they would like to see in their organization. Then make those changes happen and let them know you fulfilled their wishes." He says that you have "the biggest opportunity to shake the tree positively in your first 100 days." Your new organization wants to demonstrate to you that it will provide you with the resources you need to remove barriers that are keeping your team from being successful. Take advantage of that honeymoon period to show your direct reports that you can get things done to their benefit.

Reach out to your peers within the second or third week. On a one-on-one basis (maybe over lunch), ask them to tell you about what worked well with your predecessor, and what didn't work so well. Remember it's not your intention to dish the dirt on the person who came before you, so be mindful that it doesn't degenerate into a bad-mouthing session. (Your new coworkers could get the impression that you're a gossip even though they did all the talking.) Be clear and careful that the discussion is about how you can succeed in your new role in such a way as to help them do *their* jobs better.

Ask them to fast forward in their imaginations a month, three months, six months into the future. To their mind, what would a successful working relationship with you look like? Ask them to describe that relationship in as detailed a way as possible. How would they like to be communicated with? Via phone? Email? A personal walk down the hall? What feels responsive to them? An immediate return email? An update when the task at hand is accomplished? What might make them feel uncomfortable or worried about the work you're doing? What would make them confident?

Listen to their feedback without interrupting. And then repeat what you think you've heard so that they get that you got it. Then recruit their help in your success. You don't have to lose your dignity here, but now's not the time for false pride or posturing. You're collecting team members all around you, below, beside, and above you. And they're going to feel personally invested in ensuring your success. After all, who wants to break in your successor? They're probably tired of seeing new faces in your department. A little familiarity could be a nice change for them, too.

Remember to pay it forward. You aren't the first new manager hire. And you probably won't be the last. As your own tenure at the company lengthens, you'll start seeing new managers. And you know what they'll be thinking, starting with, "Oh please, let this be my last new job for a while."

Reach out to them. Find out whether they might be interested in hearing from someone who has successfully landed. Take them to lunch. Tell them what you've learned that works especially well in this new culture they're in. Introduce them to the more tenured managers—the ones who helped you when you started. But don't rush or judge them. Just make the offer available to them; they can take you up on it when they're ready.

Cut yourself a break. Some things are within your control. And, frankly, some things aren't.

Says Walztoni: "Stephen Covey talks about the *circle of influence* and the *circle of concern*. You can be concerned that the sword could drop again any time—and it could. It has before. But what you are really able to influence is your relationships with your manager, your peers, and the people who will work for you. You can help your people achieve the results that your organization and company needs to realize its goals. Stay with what you can influence."

The best thing you can do:
Find out what the two to three critical wins are that your organization needs from you, and deliver them. At least once a month, remember to ask for monthly feedback on your progress against its expectations. If you are achieving those goals, this will give the opportunity to notice how effective you have been.

The worst thing you can do:
Sit back, relax, and think that being laid off could never happen again.

The first thing you should do:
Be thankful for the opportunity to contribute in a new organization, and then do the preceding "best thing you can do."

Voice of Experience: Sarah

I had been with my company for 19 years and 6 months. And I was laid off by a newly installed management team while I was on vacation in Aruba. Everyone at work knew because my email address had disappeared. But I found out when my boyfriend picked me up at the airport and said, "There's a message on the machine from your manager. You will want to listen to it when you get home."

I had been grumbling about my job for a very long time. I just didn't know how to leave. It felt like I was just stuck there. But I was also extremely afraid of losing my job, and now it happened.

I realized this is what I wanted to happen all along, plus I get a package. So now I could figure out what I wanted to do. I went in the next day, and all my friends came to help me pack up. That's when it first hit me that after having been there for so many years, helping so many people, promoting people, it finally came down to, "That's it, see you later." I was let go by a bunch of people who didn't even know me.

I was angry because my friends were there. I don't have any family, so they had become my family. That was probably what bothered me more than anything else.

Even though I got a year's salary and could have taken the time to think about what I really wanted to do next, it was scary. And so I immediately made a few phone calls to former colleagues who had started a business. They needed me right away, so I jumped right into the next job. I went from a completely structured environment in my old job to a free-for-all in this new culture. I was there only ten very painful months before I quit that job. Basically, that was just the wrong job, and I had just put off the inevitable of grieving and processing through the loss of my first job.

In 18 months, I had lost a job and I quit a job. I'm now a consultant. It's not my dream job, but you know what? I don't think there is a dream job out there for me. To me a job is somewhere I can go where I can work with people I like and make things happen. So that could really be anywhere.

From a mental perspective, this whole experience strengthened me as a person. It built my character and it boosted my confidence. It took away the fears I had. I'm no longer afraid of losing my job.

The other thing that really struck me was the way losing my job changed my identity. I used to be the powerful person in the big corner office. And the people who used to fawn all over me before really have no time for me now. When I see them in the lobby, where I wait to meet a friend for lunch, they'll walk right by. When I was sitting in the big office, I was somebody. Now I have to be somebody without the big office.

If I felt I could influence change back in my old company and help people with the way I am today, I'd go back. But would I go back to the same environment and work under the same conditions? No way. I'm not that person anymore. I took a crash course in growing up in the past 18 months, that's for sure. And I don't think I ever would have done that if they hadn't thrown me out. But even today I still have the problem where I will refer to my old company as "we."

The best thing you can do:
Resist the temptation of taking the next job too quickly, if you can afford to. You need to take advantage of the downtime you've been given to rediscover yourself.

The worst thing you can do:
Blame the messenger. It's really not his fault.

The first thing you should do:
Sit down and think about the positive ways this can affect your life.

CHAPTER 26

Never Be in This Situation Again

Throughout this book, we've talked about how to deal with this current situation in your life—your career, your finances, your friends, your family, your own frame of mind. So now let's talk a little bit about your future.

There's a kind of magical thinking that surrounds catastrophe. Many of us (including me) somehow believe that once we've paid our Big Dues, nothing so bad can ever happen to us again. (Which is why, I suppose, people immediately think that they have to land another job—and fast—to rest easy in the arms of the perception of security again.) But those who have been laid off more than once will tell you that lightning does strike twice, sometimes even three or four or five times in the same spot. At least career lightning does. Through absolutely no fault of their own, other than the fact they were there.

So maybe it's time for us to shift positions—or at least our stance on what security really means to us personally. We've clearly seen that there's no promise of security in the form of the regular paycheck that comes from one source. It's okay, for the moment, but I wouldn't bet the retirement fund on it.

As I wrote in the preface, when my dedicated, talented, hardworking father was laid off, it hit me that no job is secure, no matter how smart and committed we are to our company's mission-critical objectives. No matter how we choose to approach our working years, we are all self-employed. And we've been that way for at least 30 years, if not longer.

If that's a frightening prospect to you, it doesn't have to be. It's just the way it is, and you can use this new realization as permission to finally reach for all things that fascinate and motivate you—those things that light that divine spark that we discussed earlier in the book. This is such a great time to be in touch with your dreams because we're learning the hard way that playing it safe is not playing it smart. So, we might as well play all out and go straight for those projects and passions that make us glad we're alive.

I'm thinking that before too long, the concept of being "laid off" is going to be more a matter of a state of mind than an actual fact—at least for high-performing, high achievers (like you) who know what their mission is in life and work. If you really don't ever want to be in the position of being laid off again, the only way you can achieve that is by fully embracing the fact that you're self-employed (regardless of whose name is on your check).

This might feel like early days for such a massive shift in perspective for both individuals and companies, but Lauren Doliva, Ph.D., a San-Francisco-based managing partner of Heidrick & Struggles (which is best known for its executive search services) is seeing that we are on the ground floor of a massive shift in the ways that work gets done and money gets made.

"We need to readjust our expectations about what the world of work has to offer," she says. "The way companies get work done is going to continue to change and look different very soon. Opportunities may not show up in terms of open positions so much as by projects. And so instead of looking for a place to land, perhaps the best thing to do is look for what needs to be done.

"We're at the beginning of a major transformation of how we structure work," she says. "There's an underlying change that a lot of people are feeling and trying to make sense of. It will make the world we live in as a global economy much more fluid, fast, and fascinating. Combine this trend with the new practices in social networking, and we have a shared economy around the world where things are getting done in a very collaborative way."

And companies need us still.

It may not exactly look like it right now, but there is still a War for Talent going on. And, Doliva says that the talent is still winning. Companies still desperately need your talents, passion, ideas, creativity, and commitment to stay on the cutting edge of your profession. They just might not need it full time—or forever. You can rage against that reality, or see it for the possibilities it brings you.

At this point you might be thinking, "I see where this is going— you're talking about consulting. That's all well and good for people with an entrepreneurial spirit. But I like working in teams, and I hate selling. Tried it 25 years ago. Didn't like it."

Do you like being laid off more? I'm guessing probably not.

Just as we have to rethink what it means to be fully employed by one company, it's time to rethink what it means to be self-employed. I think the term *sole proprietor* has probably become useful only for accounting purposes. None of us can operate in a vacuum, no one is sole anything—except perhaps solely responsible for paying the mortgage. We all need each other to get our jobs done and make our dreams come true, no matter how we're employed.

So how do we do that from here on out? Those of us who prefer the temporary safety of a single company and single source for the paycheck must always remember that it could come to an end any minute—quite literally, as we've been seeing. Those of us who prefer the freedom of working "for ourselves" would do well to remember that the only way we'll thrive is by plugging our talents into very real corporate needs and requirements out there in the marketplace.

And companies would do well to remember that talent comes in all packages—full-time employees and the great network of knowledge, passion, and skills represented by individuals who have chosen to go it alone. It's time for companies to improve their own chances of thriving by opening their procedures up to the individual passions of sole proprietors with really great ideas.

"Just as companies change people," says Doliva, "people change companies."

And so, instead of limiting funds only to approved job reqs, it's time for companies to open their budgets to more and more projects to get the same work done by a variety of individuals. Even, very likely, the same people who once worked for them on a full-time basis just a couple of weeks ago. Just think of the money they'll save on severance packages alone.

Of course, as I write this, I realize that I'm writing to *you* (the individual) about *them* (the companies and the individual managers who run them from within). And it hasn't escaped my notice that eventually you will most likely be one of them, as you land in your next great job working full time for a company.

When that time comes, you will one day get an email or a phone call from an individual who may have been recently laid off, or who had long ago decided that dedicated full-time self-employment was the best way to go. When you get that ping, stop what you're doing and listen to what this individual has to offer, ask, or say.

After all, that person is you, too. We're all self-employed. And we all want the same thing: to reach our full potential making our dreams come true. And maybe making the world a better place for all of us while we're at it.

PART VI

APPENDIXES

Step Away from the Fridge! Reach for This Instead

Don't you just love it when the answers are in the back of the book? How long has it been since you flipped toward the back of a book and snuck a peek for a solution? But back in algebra and geometry classes, even though the answers were in the back, they were never really entirely helpful, were they? You still had to figure out how to arrive at those answers.

Well, here's a nice surprise for you. In this case, these answers will help you get to where you want to go! We've pulled the Best Things, Worst Things, and First Things (you should do) together and arranged them here for you to quickly reference when you're feeling like you need a quick boost of encouragement. So much better than cheesecake. Well. Not really. If I could give you cheesecake, I would. Hopefully, this will come in at a close second.

The Best Things You Can Do

The Inner Game of Getting Laid Off

- Give yourself the chance to go through all the feelings that are coming your way.
- Assume success.
- Recognize that this period of layoffs—whether it actually happens to you—is just another moment in time, having nothing to do with your essential value and meaning.

Preparing for a Layoff

- Recognize that everyone is subject to being laid off.
- Think ahead and make easy but valuable changes in your financial life.
- Maintain your dignity so that you can keep your self-respect.
- Remember you're only human.
- Think about where it is you want to go. And make your choices accordingly.
- Keep your network active, no matter how comfortable you feel at your present job. It's important to build strong personal relationships with your clients and vendors.
- Be prepared. Make sure your resumé is up-to-date, and maintain your business contacts.

Know Your Rights

- Listen carefully and take excellent notes of the meeting.
- Don't take it personally, especially in situations of mass layoffs.
- Understand that the layoff process is probably driven by a mandate from the legal department.
- Assume everything is negotiable.

When You've Been Laid Off

- Give yourself time to think about where you are emotionally and what you want to do.
- Remember that you are still in control of your finances.
- Give your children the age-appropriate information they need to feel safe.
- Take action. It's extremely empowering to know that you are still in control.

Landing Your Next Job

- Assume that there are a number of opportunities for you out there. Your job is to find them because they're not going to find you.

- Assign yourself a research project, and then build up a list of all the people you would like to reach out to work with you on it.

- Keep in mind that you're a valuable connection in other people's networks.

- Create a clear plan of what you're going to do, when you're going to do it, how you're going to do it.

- Be very clear about your priorities and goals when talking with prospective employers.

- Figure out how you're relevant to the company's bottom line.

- If you're new to social networking, set aside a half day, make yourself very comfortable in front of the computer (you can even wear your pajamas for this project), and just explore the world of social networking sites.

The Worst Things You Can Do

The Inner Game of Getting Laid Off

- Judge or rush yourself as you cycle through those feelings.

- Panic and shut your mind down to opportunities and ideas.

- Accept these less-abundant times as rock-solid proof that efforts are futile and the world is a hostile, unwelcoming environment for the likes of you.

- Think it won't happen to you.

Preparing for a Layoff

- Assume it's too late to change your financial ways.
- Lose your composure out of fear or anger.
- Stress yourself out so much that you lose control.
- Burn your bridges on your way out.

Know Your Rights

- Get emotional, thereby harming your ability to negotiate.
- Sign anything without thoroughly considering your options.
- Panic.

When You've Been Laid Off

- Blame the messenger. It's really not her fault.
- Take the company's treatment of you as a reflection of how it really thinks of you.
- Get embroiled in the woulda, coulda, shoulda's so much that you're not able to move forward with your life.
- Convince yourself that you're no one without a company title.
- Act out of desperation.
- Do nothing.
- Wallow in self-pity. You have to get your mind set and clear as quickly as possible to look for another job.
- Give up on all your goals, objectives, dreams, and visions just because you've been laid off. Don't lose sight of the things that are most important in your life.
- Worry about other people's opinion of you as you start cutting expenses.

- Be a bad role model to your children for handling anxiety and depression.
- Stay angry or repress that emotion. Those two approaches will just immobilize you.

Landing Your Next Job
- Go out into the job market when you're still emotionally raw from the layoff experience.
- Waste your time by focusing just on online applications. If you see that a company has an opening that interests you, use your network to connect with someone inside the company whom you can meet directly.
- Pass out your resumé with no effort to make a sincere, personal connection with the person whose help you want.
- Sit back, relax, and think that being laid off could never happen again.
- Do things online that you wouldn't do in front of a boss in person.
- Take first job you were offered just because you were offered the job.

The First Things You Should Do

The Inner Game of Getting Laid Off
- Make a list of the things you can control positively and focus on that for now.
- Something for yourself, ideally in the company of someone you care about…and who cares about you.
- Hug someone you love and count your blessings.

Preparing for a Layoff

- Keep in mind that getting laid off has nothing to do with your performance.
- Take a ruthless look at your finances. Find fat that you can trim. Just knowing your financial situation is a big step to taking control of your life.
- Remember you're only human!

Know Your Rights

- Understand what you're signing.
- Take your time to read and fully understand the severance contract that's been presented to you.
- Know exactly what the company is offering you. Talk to someone in HR to make sure you understand what your benefits situation is so that you don't put yourself in a worse position financially by making a foolish mistake. If they offer outplacement services, use it.

When You've Been Laid Off

- Acknowledge all your feelings and emotions associated with your loss.
- Think of your friends as your support squad and remember that they want to help you. Even if they don't quite know how.
- Maintain perspective. Sklover says, "This is not hearing that you have terminal cancer or that a loved one has been in a car accident. This is something that you will survive no matter what."
- Remind yourself that most of the changes you will make are excellent money management habits during any economic period.

- Sit down, take out a pen, make a list, and then start crossing things off that you know you can immediately save money on.

- Assess your financial situation, so you don't do or say things that are panic-driven.

- Resolve to put the circumstances of the actual layoff behind you, because that memory will be the one that could hurt the most as you try to move forward in your life.

- Sit down and think about the positive ways this can affect your life.

- Remind yourself that you may have lost your job, but you haven't lost your reason for being.

- Take a deep breath, step back, and view this as a problem to be solved by your team. Your team is your family, friends, and network.

- Do something and do it right now. Take control over what is going to happen to you. Don't wait until your hand is forced. You absolutely lose your power then.

- Seek counseling, so that you're mentally and emotionally focused to do what you have to do to find another job.

- Reach out to people you care about and trust and allow them to be your support mechanism. Don't isolate yourself.

Landing Your Next Job

- Make a list of at least 101 people you know. You may hit a wall at number 35, but keep going anyway. Your brain will get the idea and start cooperating.

- Create a list of every organization that might be a potential employer. Your mission right now isn't about finding jobs. It's about finding people who hire people like you.

- Be thankful for the opportunity to contribute in a new organization.

- Immediately get the word out that you're in the market for a job. Don't let the shame or negative self-talk stop you.

- Present yourself enthusiastically. What employers are looking for is commitment.

- Find out what the two to three critical wins are that your new organization needs from you, and deliver them.

Greg and Martha's List of Automatic No's

One of the many drawbacks of being between jobs is that now you have more time to talk to people—people who couldn't even break your stride when you were busy running from one appointment and project to the next. The problem here is that these people have more time to talk to you—talk you into saying yes to so-called deals that could fritter your cash, evaporate your savings, or threaten your identity or credit rating.

You might have more time, but don't give it to these people! Don't worry about hurting their feelings with an abrupt rejection. (Remember, as smart as you are, you're outmuscled by these people. They are professionally trained to get you to listen and then say yes; you're not professionally trained to say no.) Don't even think twice about their offers and appeals. Don't stop to even think about it. Don't even stop to hear them out.

I'm the kind of person who won't even let a telemarketer draw in the first breath to begin saying, "Hey, Martha! How you doin' today?" The instant I get that I've got a telemarketer on the line, I say, "Thanks, no thanks, bye." Click. (My friends are appalled by my rudeness. Ask me if I care.) As it happened, I was feeling especially dozy a couple of days before I was slated to interview Greg Karp for Chapter 13, "Financial: Control Your Spending." And the phone rang. Caller ID said it was "*Famous Name* Publisher." Because I'm a writer and because the publishing company is quite well known, my curiosity got the better of me. So, never mind the fact it was on a Saturday when all editors I know are actually living their lives, not working, I answered the phone. Hello?

Come to find out, I was a finalist for a Brand! New! Car! And the caller only wanted to know if I preferred black or silver, should I be the actual winner. Um. Black, I suppose. (What? No red?) Okay great. I'll also be glad to know that a diamond watch is now on its way to me. (Ick. But okay.) Now, since I am a finalist, I also get a free subscription to one of the following three magazines....

By now I'm awake. And curious to see how this whole conversation would play itself out. So I let this telemarketer run my line out for at least 20 minutes before I could hear a click in her script reel and she starts to try to bring me in for the kill. Finally, she tells me that I'm also eligible for five other free subscriptions; the only thing is that they'll need me to pay for the postage/handling, just a mere $3.50 a month. ("Bring out the hook, boys! I've got a live one here!")

"Wait a minute," I interrupt her, "are you going to be asking me to give you a credit card number before this call is over?"

"Oh, I won't," she assures me, "That will be done by my supervisor."

"Sorry," I say, "I don't give my credit card information to a stranger on the phone. I'm sure you understand."

"It doesn't have to be a credit card number," she's so resourceful and considerate. "We can take your checking information over the phone."

At that point all I can do is just laugh. And I point out to her that's hardly an improvement on the security scenario. And I repeat I don't give my financial information on the phone to a stranger.

Her response: "Well, thank you very much for wasting my time, you strange lady." *And then she hangs up on me!*

And now I'm peeved. How dare someone hang up on me! And am I really a strange lady? And then how weird am I that I should be rattled by an insult from a rip-off artist? I'm peeved in so many different ways I don't know which one to start with first.

And then I remember the phone interview I have scheduled with Greg Karp! Bing! On goes the light bulb! So, after the formal interview was over, Greg and I brainstormed this list of "automatic no's." It was fun. It made me feel much better. And now we're passing it on to you!

So, just say *no* to...

- Strangers calling out of the blue asking for any financial or personal information
- Strangers asking you for help paying for surgeries or getting cash out of countries because you're the only one they can trust
- Sellers on eBay or other secure online auctions who offer you a better deal outside the auspices of the official online auction site
- Extended warranties
- Requests for charitable pledges over the phone
- Retailers, doctors, vets, and anyone who asks for your Social Security number but has no business knowing your credit-worthiness
- Credit card insurance
- Mortgage insurance
- Specific death or disease insurance
- Flight insurance
- Timeshare properties

- Any decision that must be made immediately or you'll lose out on a deal
- Every single time you don't understand something
- Bottled water
- Child life insurance
- Rental car insurance (Check in advance of the transaction to be sure that your credit card or car insurance covers car rentals.)
- Smoking
- Lottery tickets

Resources and Suggested Reading

Preface

- *We Are All Self-Employed: How to Take Control of Your Career*
  Cliff Hakim
  Berrett-Koehler Publishers, Inc., 2003

  www.rethinkingwork.com

Chapter 2

- *Your Job Survival Guide: A Manual for Thriving in Change*
  Gregory Shea and Robert Gunther
  FT Press, 2009

  www.yourjobsurvivalguide.com

Chapter 5

- Mark Gibbs
  Gibbs Financial Planning Services
  4420 South Lee Street, Suite B
  Buford, GA 30518

  770-831-8652
  mgibbs@gibbsfinancialpc.com
  www.GibbsFinancialPC.com

Chapter 6

- *Traveling Hopefully: How to Lose Your Family Baggage and Jumpstart Your Life*
  Libby Gill
  St. Martin's Griffin, 2005

- *You Unstuck*
  Libby Gill
  Solas House, 2009

  libby@libbygill.com
  www.libbygill.com

Chapters 9 and 10

- *Sklover's Guide to Job Security: The 7 Steps to Staying Employed and Staying Employable*
  Alan L. Sklover
  The 7 Steps, 2003

  Alan L. Sklover
  10 Rockefeller Plaza
  New York, NY 10020

  www.skloverworkingwisdom.com

Chapter 12

- *HR from the Heart: Inspiring Stories and Strategies for Building the People Side of Great Business*
  Libby Sartain and Martha I. Finney
  Amacom, 2003

  www.libbysartain.com
  www.hrjourneys.blogspot.com

Chapter 13

- *Living Rich by Spending Smart: How to Get More of What You Really Want*
  Gregory Karp
  FT Press, 2008

  www.gregkarp.com

Chapter 14

- Meredith Kaplan
  Meredith Kaplan Coaching
  11380 Prosperity Farms Road, Suite 217
  Palm Beach Gardens, FL 33410

  561-627-7207
  meredithkaplan@bellsouth.net
  www.meredithkaplancoaching.com

- *Destructive Emotions: How Can We Overcome Them?*
  Daniel Goleman (Editor)
  Bantam, 2004

- *Learned Optimism: How to Change Your Mind and Your Life*
  Martin Seligman
  Pocket Books, 1998

- *The Success Principles: How to Get from Where You Are to Where You Want to Be*
  Jack Canfield and Janet Switzer
  Harper Resource Book, 2005

- *Transitions*
  William Bridges
  Perseus Books, 1980

Chapter 15

- Ellen Berman, Psy.D.
  Berman & Associates
  123 MacGregor Drive
  Stamford CT 06902

  203-961-8818
  ellen@doctorberman.net
  www.doctorberman.net/CoreSkills

- *The Optimistic Child: A Proven Program to Safeguard Children from Depression and Build Lifelong Resilience*
  Martin Seligman
  Mariner Books, 2007

Chapter 17

- Bill Berman, Ph.D.
  Berman & Associates
  123 MacGregor Drive
  Stamford CT 06902

  203-961-8818
  bill@doctorberman.net
  www.doctorberman.net/CoreSkills

- *Making a Good Brain Great*
  Daniel G. Amen
  Three Rivers Press, 2005

Chapter 18

- *Power Networking, 2nd Edition: 59 Secrets for Personal & Professional Success*
  Donna Fisher
  Bard Press, 2000

Donna Fisher
1415 S. Voss Road, Ste. 110-138
Houston, TX 77057

713-789-2484
donna@donnafisher.com
www.donnafisher.com

Chapter 19

- *The Truth About Profiting from Social Networking*
  Patrice-Anne Rutledge
  FT Press, 2008

  patrice@patricerutledge.com
  www.patricerutledge.com

Chapter 21

- Duncan Mathison, M.S.
  10802 Melva Road
  La Mesa, Ca 91941

  duncan@duncanmathison.com
  www.duncanmathison.com

Chapter 22

- Jeffrey Saltzman
  Principal, Kenexa

  914-747-7736
  http://blog.kenexa.com/blogdetails.aspx?u=11
  www.linkedin.com/in/jeffreysaltzman
  jeffrey.saltzman@kenexa.com

Chapter 23

- *Bargaining for Advantage: Negotiation Strategies for Reasonable People*
  G. Richard Shell
  Penguin, 2006

  shellric@wharton.upenn.edu
  www.wharton.upenn.edu/faculty/shellric.html

Chapter 25

- Mark Walztoni
  5 Remedios Road,
  Santa Fe, NM 87540

  505-466-2695
  mark@markwalztoni.com
  www.markwalztoni.com

- *The First 90 Days: Critical Success Strategies for New Leaders at All Levels*
  Michael Watkins
  Harvard Business School, 2003

Chapter 26

- Lauren Doliva, Ph.D.
  Managing Partner, Chief Advisor Network
  Heidrick & Struggles
  One California Street, Suite 2400
  San Francisco, CA 94111

  chiefadvisornetwork@heidrick.com
  www.heidrick.com

Index

A

"A" player status, building, 120-124
accepting
    job offers, 142-147
        case study: Deborah, 145-146
        when not to negotiate, 142-144
    layoff news gracefully, 32-33
adjusting expectations about job
    security, 156-159
Alice in Wonderland (Lewis), 10
alienation following a layoff, 7
Ally McBeal, 38
apologizing for poor reaction, 40-41
asking for special treatment, 56-58
Association for Women in
    Communications, 108
automatic no's, 170-173

B

Ball, Lucille, 40
*Bargaining for Advantage: Negotiation
    Strategies for Reasonable People*
    (Shell), 143
Berman, Bill, 102-105
Berman, Ellen Raynes, 88-90
bewilderment following a layoff, 7
Blake, William, 12
breaking habits, 30
bungled and poorly managed
    layoffs, 64-66

C

cable television, reducing spending
    on, 73
career realities and rules, 10
    dependence on transient
        relationships, 13-14
    embracing insecurity, 10-12
    keeping yourself valuable in
        changing market, 12-13
    training for disaster, 14-15

Carroll, Lewis, 10
Carter administration, federal layoffs
    during, xvi
case studies
    Anna, 82-84
    Caroline, 42-44
    Charles, 93-95
    Deborah, 145-146
    Rob, 23-25
    Sarah, 152-154
    Simon, 96-97
cash, saving, 29
cell phone, reducing spending on,
    74
children, telling about layoff, 30,
    86-90
circle of concern, 151
circle of influence, 151
COBRA, 29
commitments, avoiding, 51
concern, circle of, 151
confidence
    organizational confidence
        external, 134
        internal, 133-134
    personal confidence
        external, 135-136
        internal, 134-135
    starting new jobs with
        confidence, 148-151
conflicting emotions, handling, 76
    case study: Anna (commissioned
        salesperson), 82-84
    tips and strategies, 79-82
    types of emotions, 76-78
connections. *See* networking
consulting, 123
contractual promises, claiming, 57
control, finding within yourself,
    16-19
controlling spending. *See* costs,
    cutting

T

talents, as asset when job hunting, 122
teachable moments from layoffs
  case study: Charles (accountant/comptroller), 93-95
  case study: Simon (survivor of two layoffs), 96-97
  list of, 92-93
telecommunications costs, reducing, 73-74
telemarketers, saying "no" to, 170-173
telling children about layoff, 86-90
term life insurance, 28
thank-you notes, 112
theme song, giving yourself, 38-39
thought leader, becoming, 121
training for disaster, 14-15
transient relationships, dependence on, 13-14
The Truth About Profiting from Social Networking (Rutledge), 115

U-V-W

understanding your rights. See knowing your rights

Vaill, Peter, 11
Vonage, 74

Walztoni, Mark, 148-151
WARN Act (Worker Adjustment and Retraining Notification Act), 65
We Are All Self-Employed (Hakim), xvii
Web pages, as asset when job hunting, 121
what to expect after a layoff
  alienation, 7
  bewilderment, 7
  crisis in self-worth, 7
  isolation, 8
  mixed feelings, 6
  overview, 4-6

when to say no, 170-173
Winfrey, Oprah, 40
Worker Adjustment and Retraining Notification Act (WARN Act), 65
workplace violence, 51

X-Y-Z

Xing.com, 115

Your Job Survival Guide (Shea), 14

FT Press

FINANCIAL TIMES

In an increasingly competitive world, it is quality
of thinking that gives an edge—an idea that opens new
doors, a technique that solves a problem, or an insight
that simply helps make sense of it all.

We work with leading authors in the various arenas
of business and finance to bring cutting-edge thinking
and best-learning practices to a global market.

It is our goal to create world-class print publications
and electronic products that give readers
knowledge and understanding that can then be
applied, whether studying or at work.

To find out more about our business
products, you can visit us at www.ftpress.com.